Mayan Civilization

An Essay on the Collapse of Mayan Civilization

(Explore the History and Mystery of the Ancient Mayan Ruins)

Cherly Guzman

Published By **Ryan Princeton**

Cherly Guzman

All Rights Reserved

Mayan Civilization: An Essay on the Collapse of Mayan Civilization (Explore the History and Mystery of the Ancient Mayan Ruins)

ISBN 978-1-77485-533-1

No part of this guidebook shall be reproduced in any form without permission in writing from the publisher except in the case of brief quotations embodied in critical articles or reviews.

Legal & Disclaimer

The information contained in this ebook is not designed to replace or take the place of any form of medicine or professional medical advice. The information in this ebook has been provided for educational & entertainment purposes only.

The information contained in this book has been compiled from sources deemed reliable, and it is accurate to the best of the Author's knowledge; however, the Author cannot guarantee its accuracy and validity and cannot be held liable for any errors or omissions. Changes are periodically made to this book. You must consult your doctor or get professional medical advice before using any of the suggested remedies, techniques, or information in this book.

Upon using the information contained in this book, you agree to hold harmless the Author from and against any damages, costs, and expenses, including any legal fees potentially resulting from the application of any of the information provided by this guide. This disclaimer applies to any damages or injury caused by the use and application, whether directly or indirectly, of any advice or information presented, whether for breach of contract, tort, negligence, personal injury, criminal intent, or under any other cause of action.

You agree to accept all risks of using the information presented inside this book. You need to consult a professional medical practitioner in order to ensure you are both able and healthy enough to participate in this program.

Table Of Contents

INTRODUCTION 1

CHAPTER 1: THE ORIGINS OF THE MAYAN PEOPLE 8

CHAPTER 2: TIKAL, THE CAPITAL CITY 18

CHAPTER 3: MAYANS AT THEIR HIGHEST AND THE DAILY LIFE 27

CHAPTER 4: ASTRONOMY AND RECORD-KEEPING 40

CHAPTER 5: THE MAYAN CALENDAR MAYAN CALENDAR 50

CHAPTER 6: GODS AND RELIGION 61

CHAPTER 7: WHAT'S THE REASON FOR THEIR DECLINE? 74

CHAPTER 8: WHAT HAPPENED TO THE MAYA PERFORM HUMAN SACRIFICE? 83

CHAPTER 9: THE EARLY SETTLERS 90

CHAPTER 10: GOLDEN AGE OF MONUMENTS 96

CHAPTER 11: THE MAYA HIGHLANDS ... 102

CHAPTER 12: THE SPANISH CONQUEST 107

CHAPTER 13: THE PREST-RULERS 110

CHAPTER 14: RELIGIOUS PRACTICES 163

CONCLUSION 183

Introduction

The expression "Mayan people" is a reference to the prehistoric civilization in Central America that peaked around the first millennium of the century, however, it also refers an era-old civilization that has spread all over the world. The Mayan civilization, in contrast to what is depicted in the media, was not never unified. It was composed of a number of smaller states, in which rulers reigned, with each state was centered around a city. Sometimes, the more powerful of the states of the Maya culture were able to be dominant or take over states that were weaker, and benefit from the efforts of the state that was weaker.

The features shared by Mesoamerican Civilizations from the Time:

It had some traits that were shared by other civilizations of Mesoamerica such as Aztecs Zapotec as well as the Olmen peoples, however, they also featured distinct characteristics that were unique to the Mayan peoples. For instance that the Mayan people had the only and only system of writing that represented the language they were speaking. The other cultures of the were using writing that was pictographic and it was the Mayan inhabitants were the sole one that had a system of writing that was developed. In reality, many aspects of this culture were improved or refined in a way other cultures did not possess.

While the other cultures of in the past shared similar designs of art and architecture however, the Maya appeared to be the most beautiful. Because of the advanced networks used that allowed trade, all the cultures of Mesoamerica were influenced by one another. In this intro, we'll briefly outline certain unique aspects of their culture. They will be explored in greater depth in the chapters in this book.

Geography of the Areas occupied by the Maya:

The Mayan people lived in the southern part of Mexico and in the Northern region that is Central America, including Belize, Honduras, El Salvador Honduras, Belize, El Salvador and Guatemala. This area also includes the central lowlands of the south, the southern highlands and the northern lowlands. These areas are home to forests, savannas, swampy regions, plateaus, and peaks. Due to the diversity of these areas, a variety of different species of plants and animals were found in these areas and the Mayan culture the Maya adjusted to this diversity in an inventive manner.

The Mayan Religion and Spirituality Mayan People:

The faith that was practiced by the Mayans was based around time as well as the cycles that accompany it, which celebrated the perpetual stage of birth to unavoidable death and finally to the rebirth. The ceremonies used by the Mayans were devoted to the cycles of this earth and celestial bodies that the priests of the time were adept at deciphering as well as understanding. Their culture was heavily dependent upon corn (maize) as well as the corn god was for them, of vital importance and significance in their daily lives. Religion was essential and central to their daily rituals and beliefs. The rituals of the Maya could be viewed by people of today with shock, as they could be very brutal.

The Unusual Architecture Of Mayan Civilization:

Great temples, pyramids and huge tombs were the main attractions in every city that was which was inhabited by Mayan people. A city at one time was inhabited by the Maya can be easily identified by their unique pyramidal building style, stepped blocks lined with luxurious grand palaces and huge plazas designed for the kings and nobles. There was one particular ritual of the religion in common with the majority of people of this region that was a particular kind of ball game which was referred to as sacred. The court used for the game was designed to be near the temples. The ancient Greeks also created the concept of corbelled archways, which allow rooms to have a soaring and light feeling that gave their palaces as well as temples an exquisite and unique elegance.

Was Mayan Civilization Collapse? Mayan Civilization Collapse, and What caused it?

While many sources and stories claim to be false however, the civilization of Maya was not wiped out completely. While some of the cities were once inhabited by them were abandoned more than 1000 years in the past, there were new cities that appeared to conquer. In the 16th century, Spaniards came to conquer the Mayans. They brought diseases that eventually had negative effects on the indigenous people of the region. Additionally the Spaniards forced the Mayan people turn to Christianity and destroyed their religious books and texts. This is the reason why there are so few Mayan remains in the present day.

However the fact that some records survived and are referred to as codices. Based on this, we are able to uncover some gaps in our knowledge of the lost civilization and learn from their way of life. We can learn what life was like for the average person, and also the kind of food they ate as well as the animals they kept. We also have a basic understanding regarding their systems of governance and also the fact that women were a key part of their communities. All this plus more, is covered in this informative guide and you're bound to learn somethingnew!

It is the Mayan People who remain in our Modern Day:

However, the people who were ancestors of the Mayans remain in existence today and can be located all over the world. Millions of living Maya around the globe and this includes Central America where they originally existed. They are not a single community, ethnic group or a single entity. They speak and understand multiple languages, which include English and Spanish along with those of the Mayan languages. However, the remaining Maya are considered to be indigenous and remain rooted to their ancestral roots in addition to more recent developments from the past century.

The numerous fascinating facts about the intriguing Mayan people will cause one to think about how they lived everyday life like for their people as well as a myriad of other fascinating facts. What would lead an incredibly successful society to total destruction? What ways did they fall behind, despite appearing to be advanced in the same way? What aspects of their culture existed prior to the time they inherited it? What made people believed in the idea that this world would be set to come to an end in the month of December of 2012? In this book, you'll discover the ancient origins of this civilization that was spread across many cities. You will also learn the factors that made these people distinct and what was eventually made of them.

Thank you for buying this book. You've made the right selection, and I'm hoping you will enjoy it!

Chapter 1: The Origins Of The Mayan

People

Humans were around before the Mayan people were born however, something about this civilization enabled them to experience progress in a way which other cultures have not even imagined. The majority of this remains hidden from view, as numerous artifacts from the past such as books and sacred texts were destroyed. But clues still remain. What can we discover from Maya culture from Maya from the clues we have left? What was it about the foundations of Maya that provided them with the distinct advantage over other peoples?

The importance of efficient farming in the flourishing Mayans: Mayans:

General hunter-gatherers were common throughout The Central area of America throughout the last millennium. While they were prevalent but the time period that is known as the Pre-classic era is when the idea of permanent villages began to grow. The preclassic period was the reason for truly efficient farmingthat allowed villages to be populated in a dense manner and was observed all over the region that Mayan inhabitants lived. The farming process became more efficient at this point due to the more robust and efficient variety of corn and the method of making it. This technique involved taking the corn and soaking it with lime juice (or similar) followed by cooking it. This increased the nutritional value of corn in terms of nutrition by an exponential amount.

The influence of other societies in the Mayans:

In this period in the Mayan people were heavily influenced from a certain group of people living in the west. They were referred to as Olmec people. Olmec people. The Olmec people could be the first to develop this calendar, which would later later become close to being synonymous with "Mayan". Furthermore recent discovery of a place used for rituals goes back to 1000 B.C. This finding provides additional information concerning the Olmec culture and the Mayans and their connection with each other, which appears to have been quite complicated. There were significant shifts in social structure that were triggered by neighbouring regions interfering with each other.

However do you think the Olmec really influence individuals from Mayan culture? While this may seem like an appropriate assumption with respect to the evidence, it appears like the entire area (including those of the Olmec as well as the Maya) underwent an evolution simultaneously changing to ways of life and ceremonies that were identical. It appears as that the Maya weren't receiving this level of innovations until centuries later from other cultures, however the developments made by the Mayans may have come from a place called Ceibal or someplace similar.

Ceibal and the significance of is the significance of this New Discovery Points to: The oldest known site of a ceremonial ceremony in the history of the Mayans was discovered within the lower regions in Central America, and appears to be around 200 years older than the other sites found in the region. The plaza, known as Ceibal and only found recently, could have been used for the purpose of observing the sun and for performing rituals. It was discovered alongside pyramids. This discovery suggests that what we believed we were aware of about the Maya could be incorrect. The evidence suggests that the culture that was the Mayans being much more complicated than we first believed. Researchers debate about whether these ancient civilizations that are most well-known for their calendar system evolved on their own or were influenced by an earlier advanced culture. The new evidence suggests the latter option; however, it's neither.

The oldest compound for Ritualistic Behaviours:

Scientists have discovered evidence of the existence of ancient dwellings and houses in the area of Ceibal. The oldest layers of this area were covered with metres upon meters of dirt, as well as more modern constructions and homes. The new evidence comes from more than 10 years of digging on this site Ceibal located within Guatemala that was habitable for 2 millennia. Finding the first structures within these layers was not an easy task because of the hundreds and years worth of work that had blocked the ways. The structures that were found recently, that existed in the early times they have a huge plaza with a structure on the western side , and an elevated platform on the eastern end. This is a pattern that is familiar to people who study Maya sites and can be seen in the middle of Olmec structures near and along the Gulf coast of the modern day Mexico.

A mysterious change that affected The Entire Region:

Researchers who discovered this utilized the method of dating known as radiocarbon to determine the year it was built and also when the year 1000 B.C. comes up. Because the date of construction is around 1000 B.C., the structures on the Ceibal site seem to be several decades older than Olmec structures along the gulf coast. This implies that the building by the Olmec may not have been Mayan-inspired. Instead, it appears like the entire region was undergoing a change in the midst of this time, with cultures from these regions borrowing from one their practices of ritual and building and changing them to come to their own distinct variations.

It is believed that the Olmec inhabitants had an earlier center that experienced an end-of-life around 1150 B.C. But, the people who lived at the time were not believed to have constructed these distinctive structures to perform ceremonial activities. In the year 800 B.C. or about that time at the time, the Mayan people who lived at the Ceibal site had changed their platform to look like an elongated pyramid. The foundation was set up until it was over 30 feet tall in the year 700.

The beginning of a Civilization:

The development of the civilization of the Maya people was long before they began to develop writing on a scale as well as before they began using their well-known calendar method. This is why there's nothing to be learned about the beliefs of the ancient Maya people. The plaza and the pyramid site could be used for rituals and rituals, which is logical. In these excavations numerous axes were discovered. They are which are believed to have been put in the area to serve as sacrifices to the gods.

The location in Ceibal to observe solar activity:

The design of the architecture here was referred to as "group-E" construction. These structures are found throughout Maya's houses and were used as solar observatories. From a west-facing perspective from a viewing point, one could observe an imposing pyramid, or the platforms in the east, which has posts at the ends and to the middle. At the time of the summer solstices every year the sun rises directly over the market towards the north. Also, during the equinoxes in spring and autumn and summer, the sun rises just in the middle close to the marker at the middle. When winter's solstice approaches the sun would rise in the south.

The first people to settle in the region of Ceibal had an idea of the construction of villages which was sophisticated. The evolution of hunting methods to the lifestyle of horticulture to living in a single location and using agriculture all took place very quickly. It is difficult to determine what drove people like the Maya people living on the plains from their largely settled lifestyles to cities and villages for the rest of their lives. One possibility is that the cultivation of corn began to increase at a rapid rate around 1000 B.C.

The Benefit Of The Olmec Over the Maya:

The inhabitants of the coast and the coast, known as the Olmec were already mastering this quickly, because they enjoyed fertile rivers close to the Gulf. The lowlands in the Mayan's region were, however, not as moist and much less fertile and contained fewer fowl as well as fish that they Olmec people probably used to supplement what they consumed. If the cultivation of corn increased in productivity around 1100 B.C., this could have forced people of the Mayan population to settle down more in one place instead of having to wander around for so long. In this period it would have made sense to cut down forests in the lowland region and focus on a way of life which was based on agriculture to ensure their existence and the ability to flourish.

In-progress Research in the Area and what it might mean:

Researchers from this area are trying to understand the surrounding environment to gain more understanding of the climate and weather in the area during the period of settlement. What can be concluded in the present, as experts believe is that the civilisation of the Maya did not necessarily arise out of an earlier civilization and failed, as was initially thought. The research being conducted at the area aren't just concerned with Maya specifically. Maya in particular, they are also rather how society generally evolves and changes over the passage of time and influences. The research findings from Ceibal indicate that new cultures aren't required to emerge out from the degrading structures of earlier cultures. They could be created through social interaction and exchange of knowledge.

There's always more to discover and learn about the past:

The thing this research is reminding us of are the amount of information that remain buried there. There's so much to learn about our own tale of evolution and development, including the evolution of Maya. It is possible that new research will come out in the coming years to prove everything we believed we knew about the Maya but only the time will reveal.

Chapter 2: Tikal, The Capital City

To be aware of any civilization looking at the capital of their city is crucial and what else can be learned regarding the city that was the capital of the Mayans? The present-day region of the world that is known as Guatemala was previously called Tikal, a city that was once a part that was part of the Mayan people. Tikal was the capital of the Mayan people. in the period of 600 B.C. until around 800 A.D. or so, according to estimates. It began modestly, with only the smallest of buildings, it then became a mighty city-state in the Maya with more than 20 pyramids of different sizes. Let's explore additional characteristics, which provide an accurate representation of the values that the Maya believed in.

Tikal The Capital Waterhole City of the Maya:

The city's name, Tikal, translates to the notion of being close to an water source and is the result of a Mayan name. The early inhabitants of the city did not call it that however, because Tikal was named prior to the time that the city was destroyed.

Nowadays, this region is one of the largest sites of excavations across Central America. It is also protected by a park dubbed Tikal National Park. Tikal National Park. Its highest point is between 682-909 A.D., Tikal existed in a space of approximately 50 miles. Tikal had a population estimated to be 100,000 inhabitants, with trade on an external scale which was the main reason for this phenomenal expansion. Recent research has revealed that the residents of the city created an elaborate system of managing water, which allowed them to thrive and to survive even in the absence of any rainfall.

The influence of a neighboring city on Tikal:

As with other cities that were inhabited by Mayans in the past, the inhabitants of Tikal used a system of writing called the glyptic method. The system employed perishable material (from bark of trees, which is now rotting away) as well as stone to write on. Researchers of this system were able to translate a lot of the written documents as well as, in addition to the findings of excavations and discoveries, they learned many things about the history of the city. In the early years of Tikal's existence it was under the influence of and perhaps even under the authority of Teotihuacan the nearby urban region.

This region was located in Mexico in the center of the country that was several hundred miles further away (about 600). Writings from the Mayans describes this city as the cattail reed that is glyph-based and paintings of artwork from Teotihuacan depict a god of rain and were discovered within the town of Tikal. It is possible to determine that Teotihuacan's city Teotihuacan through a written record from 379 A.D. The record says that a ruler was able to the top of Tikal and was depicted carrying a spear and wearing feathers and shells (all belonging to the connected with the Teotihuacan individuals).

Constructions and Double Pyramids

The awe-inspiring, and famous pyramids was influenced, at the very least in part from the Maya calendar. Maya people. In the 672 years that followed A.D., rulers of the city would construct an array of twin pyramids in the final days of each 20 years. The structures feature a flat top and they were built in conjunction with the others, and contained the staircases that were on either one side. Between the pyramids, there was an enormous plaza with structures that were built from the northern region towards the south.

An early example of this structure was built by an individual named Ah Cacau. He was one of the rulers of the time. The structure consisted of a house constructed on the southern end that was adorned with nine entrance structures. In the northern part there's an enclosure with an altar within. In total, there were nine double pyramids discovered inside the capital of Tikal. It seems that they were built to the point that Tikal came to an end.

It is the Northern Acropolis Area:

When the city was just beginning to emerge there was an area which was used to place the remains of high-end citizens of Tikal especially the rulers and kings. This is the area that lies in the north and is also known as"the "North Acropolis". This region is an intricate collection of shrines, tombs, and temples. They have been constructed and rebuilt many times throughout the time of

Tikal. They cover more than three acres and are full of history about the high society of Tikal.

Special Temple Pyramids specifically designed for Ancient rulers from Tikal:

In addition to the double pyramids rulers from Tikal could also construct pyramids that could be used as temples. Six of them were built as a symbol of the burial location of rulers. There are two of them, that are referred to as temple I as well as Temple II which are seated on opposite sides of the. They are located in the central area of Tikal and feature a magnificent plaza in between them.

* Temple 1: This is the initial temple is located on the east and is 145 feet high. The stairwell traverses a number of layers that are organized in nine steps for each. These steps take visitors to a room which is located at the top of the stairs . It illustrates the people it was designed for an important ruler called Jasaw Kaan K'awil. This ruler led the troops from Tikal to defeat the enemies of Calakmul which was their biggest rival. The burial place of the ruler was found in the middle of the pyramid and included a

variety of expensive objects, including jade as well as jaguar's pelts as well as intricate artwork that was carved into human bones.

* Temple II: The next pyramid, which is located next to Temple I and is referred to as Temple II, is thought to be built for the wife of the ruler who this first temple was constructed for. The city she was from was close to and in the southeast. The marriage of her is believed to strengthen an alliance on which it was founded. The marriage pyramid called Temple II, is 125 calls and was constructed with three distinct levels of steps. On the top of the structure is a way to enter and a carving of an image of a woman in the wood. She is dressed wearing a regal bonnet, but the design in the present times is badly worn.

Its Ancient Palace Area:

As you head to the south from the temples mentioned above, you'll come close to Tikal's Palace. Tikal and is also known by the name of Central Acropolis. Like those of Northern Acropolis depicted earlier, the area has expanded and been added to numerous times throughout the history of Tikal. The palace was used in the beginning, starting about 375 A.D. The palace, which was smaller in comparison, was equipped with stairs in both the western and eastern areas and benches made out of stone. These benches could have been utilized by rulers to lie on while doing their business, and would have been covered with pelts of animals to create a more comfortable stone. Through time, the palace developed into a complex structure with at least six areas for courtyards and an irrigation reservoir in the south. This is a further proof how the Mayan inhabitants were big admirer of pyramids. In the southern region of the complex is a five-level palace. levels, which creates an appearance like the appearance of a pyramid. It is topped off with a set of stairs that let visitors explore the area. On the eastern side of the structure is a viewing platform that was constructed to watch over the court that was used for the ball game mentioned earlier in the book. The game is believed have been played with balls made from rubber, however it isn't clear what rules were used to us today. We know it was the rule of the ruler as well as his household members, enjoyed the privilege of having a prime seat at the table.

The Complex of the Lost Mayan World:

The first known pyramid in Tikal, the city that was once capital of Tikal began around two millennia back, and continued to be modified to A.D., at about the 4th century. In the fourth century, the structure was more than 100 feet high. Archaeologists today describe this amazing site as being"the "Lost world" structure. The complex is located just to the southwest of the two temples we discussed prior to this section. The burial grounds in the vicinity indicate that the site was used in the past to bury the Tikal's most prestigious citizens.

The downfall from the Great City of Tikal:

It is impossible to understand all the details about the an ancient Mayan civilization however we can state that Tikal, the Capital city Tikal along with large parts of Maya civilization is believed to have fallen into ruins. It happened around 990 A.D. However some cities, such as the city in northern Chichen Itza, flourished long after Tikal was over. Why then did Tikal fall apart after having been extravagant and lavish? It is a question which is a hot topic of discussion.

What was the cause of the city's eviction? of Tikal?

There is evidence that points towards a drought that destroyed the city since maritime trade routes could not have been feasible. Furthermore it appears that the forest may be shrinking as the city expanded in the size. This may be a factor in the problem and made rainfall less frequent and causing a more difficult time for crop growth. It is interesting to note that after the residents of Tikal left this area thriving forest emerged to take over the terrain, encasing the entire area in lush foliage.

Chapter 3: Mayans At Their Highest And

The Daily Life

What was the time when people of the Mayan population at its highest? Experts think that these rich cultures attained their peak during the centuries between the time of the year 250 A.D. and the year 990 A.D. This time period is described by archaeologists as a classic time, including multiple cities of the Mayan people, which flourished across the entirety of Central America. The Mayan people seem to have reached levels of intellectual and artistic pursuits that were far superior to those of other nations. Only a handful of areas within Europe might even match their achievements. The advancements were accompanied by huge populations, an effective and thriving economic structure and the use of trade to boost growth. This all reflects the period known as the classic. It was also a common occurrence during this time.

The Many Cities of the Mayan World:

As we have mentioned in the book, there's no single entity or ethnic group who is the Maya. They are, and were in fact, more complex than that, and have across a number of cities. Each city has distinct characteristics that made them distinct from one and the other. Here are a few of the most notable Mayan cities:

* Tikal The Capital of Pyramids The capital city of Tikal that we discussed in the last chapter was the highest-ranked when it came to building pyramids. They started this process early in the 672 year A.D. They demonstrated great order within their buildings, adhering to the pre-determined plans for structuring their pyramids and complexes.

* Palenque The Limestone City: This site is another city in the Maya was renowned for its sculpture made of limestone. It also featured the magnificent burial of King (Pakal) in one of their pyramids. The king's death was a cause for celebration, and his funeral included as many as six others, who were offered as sacrifices in an edifice stuffed with jade. He was dressed in a mask made of jade, too. The tomb wasn't

discovered until 1952. It has been described as an American discovery that rivals that of the King's tomb. Tut.

* Copan * Copan, the Hieroglyphic temple site It was located in the present-day Honduras and is famous for its temple, which has the stairway of hieroglyphs. The structure is like the pyramid, that was constructed and decorated with thousands of symbols. The glyphs are located on a staircase that is made up of more than 60 steps. This is significant since they are the largest inscription from the ancient Mayans known. Additionally, the inscription is important due to the fact that it is believed to tell an intricate story about the rulers who once lived in the city.

The distinctions that set these cities apart show that even though the Maya is a term meant to encompass a large number of people however, they were distinctly distinct from each other in terms of skill and character. However, certain features were shared by all the cities, and were distinct Mayan.

The Daily Life of different social classes of Mayan People:

Similar to how other cultures from the Mesoamerican time period operated in the same way, how a typical citizen's life was lived was largely influenced with their social class on a social scale. The way you lived your life was much better when you were in the upper tier in the hierarchy of food and you had to put in a lot of effort when you were at the lowest. Let's look at who was in these various categories of Maya:

The top class Social class members were divided into several groups, with the highest being noble families and the rulers (kings). The majority of nobles served as priests or distinguished warriors or officials of the state or Scribes.

* Middle Class: The group consisted of potters, warriors weavers, as well as professional traders. The Mayan culture Mayan people was heavily dependent on agriculture and crops for food and trading. This meant that a majority of Mayan farmers tended to their crops during the growing season. After the harvest season was over many of them went back to work to build the massive cities of the Mayan civilization.

"The Commoners" of Mayan Culture:
A typical day for the commoner who was Maya included a lot of physical work. It's not to say that they did not live happy or content lives. The farmers' families did not live in a shabby manner, and they always consumed delicious food. Their work each day brought their families food and whatever was leftover was given to other people.

* The jobs of female Commoners: Women mostly worked at the home milling maize (corn) as well as cooking food, caring for children and tending the gardens and tending the beehives. They also made cloths to make clothes for wear and also to sell.

* Jobs for Commoners of Males Men and boys, usually were tenders in fields where beans, squash and corn were grown. The principal crop here was obviously corn, but aside from that there were other crops that grew. Some of these were onions, garlic and papaya, avocados, chili peppers, tomatoes and sweet potatoes too.

Animals for Families of Common-folk Maya:

Certain families in the past were known to keep livestock like dogs, turkeys, or ducks. The hunters would typically hunt wild pigs as well as deer, and also went fishing in nearby lakes, oceans and rivers. Apart from farming, common people could have been employed as transportation workers for limestone, as porters or even as servants to the wealthy. The majority of people had the task of farming. There were no animals available to assist in plowing or carrying the load like oxen or horses, which meant it was men to complete the work. The Mayans didn't use any metals, but rather relied upon flint and obsidian for jobs that required sharp tools.

A typical day for the common family of Mayan Farmers:

The family members of Mayan farmers typically day, start their work at a very early time. With mats made of reeds, the whole family (including the extended family members) would share a bed in a home with only one room. Breakfasts were typically comprised of a kind of porridge made with cornmeal, water, chili peppers or honey to flavor. Men and boys would wear loincloths as well as the occasionally a cape to keep warm during colder winter days. Women and girls generally wore long skirts with basic blouses. After eating their breakfast, women began making pottery or weaving as the males and boys went away to work in the fields around them.

Throughout the day, boys and men would eat meals composed from dumplings filled with corn metal, vegetables, and corn. When their day at work was done, they could go home to spend time with their families. When everyone returned from work, family members would get together to eat their main meal, which was dinner. The meal was typically comprised of tortillas made made of cornmeal, stuffed with vegetables and meat, and sometimes even fish. Then , the family members would lay down to sleep when the sun set.

Unpaid Time to the Maya Common People:
However, living in the Maya was not just about work. Every month, around, an major festival to celebrate religious holidays would take place in the capital city where people would gather to dance, pray to gods and

sing. Children of the Maya civilization wouldof course enjoy playing around with their toy just like children everywhere. These celebrations also included delicious food suppers that included delicious food. After eating, the residents might have enjoyed ball games, which could be a religious ceremony for reasons, or just for entertainment and enjoyment of those watching.

More information about the role that Mayan Women Played in Ancient Times.

Mayan Women in Ancient Times:

As archaeologists studied Maya culture from the past, they frequently thought that males were viewed to be superior within these communities, and women were seen as subordinates. This seemed to be in line with the evidence collected at the time as there wasn't any reason for the time being, to question this. The assumption was that the positions of king and ruler in cities was reserved for males and that in homes and family, men also had the power to rule. Research conducted in more recent times haven't really done much to disprove this notion. But, recent studies have confirmed that females played a much more important role in the societies we believed.

The female city rulers from The Mayan Era:

In during the Mayan Classical era happened, certain females were in charge in specific cities and serve as the governing force. In general, this meant acting as regents for the son of a father who was not yet old enough or for a widow of a ruler who passed away without allowing the successor in the position. Females were also employed in the past in the role of priestesses, of an oral nature in various locations that were considered sacred. In the economics of the Maya females were also present, as being involved in agriculture zones and textiles. There is no doubt that the majority of Mayan women occupied traditional roles, primarily as domestic workers, but there were some who held higher-profile and powerful roles in the past.

While it was not common for women to be heavily involved in the political life within Mayan society, it was possible that there could sometimes be instances that resulted in the female as the ruler. Females were able to acquire more influence in politics during the time called the classical period when norms were changed and became more complex. Females were rarely involved in hierarchical religious structures However, more recent evidence suggests that female priestesses during the time called Post-Classical. This was based on evidence, in the vicinity of Yucatan.

Women Priestesses, Diviners and Females on Pilgrimage Sites:

Within this region are caves, which the Mayans believed were sacred sites for sacrifices. They were popular sites to commemorate the gods, and attracted the top members of Maya societies, as well as the more common people. These were holy places and the goddesses were often used as their inspiration which included moon goddesses and fertility goddess. These places were where priestesses would lead the pilgrims on the paths to make the purpose of pilgrimage. Sometimes, women would also act as diviners or fortune tellers for travelers.

The role of women In Mayan Economic Matters:

Females were employed in various agricultural roles like herding and farming, however they also played the role as well, of producing textiles to be used in the economy. This was for the market and trading networks on a smaller scale. They were weavers, dyers and spinners who produced cloth that provided family members with clothing. They also created elaborate pieces of art by using textiles. Most of the food that was grown and handled by Maya was consumed in the local area However, there were some items that were widely traded for example, cacao and vanilla beans. In some areas where women were raising herds of deerand making sure there was a sufficient amount of deer to keep the population well-fed. Women's work in agriculture and textiles made invaluable contributions to the business of Mayan people.

The General Economic and Political Power of the Mayan People:

Food gathering and general agricultural activities were the mainstays in the lives of the Mayans but they also had a sophisticated economy that could sustain specialists, trade routes and professional traders. This civilization did not develop the traditional minted version of currency, however they did have other items for currency, including cacao beans, copper bells and specific varieties of bread. This showed how creative and resourceful these society were of Mayan individuals were. The power of kings had was mostly dependent on the extent to which they were able to manage their resources.

The Importance of Controlling Resources for Mayan King and Rulers:

The control and management of resources pumped so much to the king's power The leaders of Mayan times governed both the production and distribution of goods that could enhance their position of authority and the status of their rulers. Additionally rulers also controlled other goods that were not local however, were needed by everyday typical Mayan families, like salt.

As time went by, Mayan rulers took over greater and greater pieces of the economic structure. The laborers of these Mayan cities were required to pay an income tax on their palaces and also the construction of temples and public works. People who were able to win battles were able limit the number of laborers. They could also use defeated citizens to pay the payment. This contributed to their strength and power economically, but even more.

Chapter 4: Astronomy And Record-Keeping

The Mayans are most well-known for their superior records and their knowledge as well as the calendar, obviously. They were a people with a culture that was more sophisticated than other cultures of the time, and included the complex and impressive language made up of hieroglyphs. What are the unique characteristics of their sophisticated knowledge and tools? Let's review some of the most notable cases of this.

A complex writing System and folding Books:

In a previous chapter in the earlier chapter, the Mayan people developed an alphabet system that was so complex that it could represent the language they used to communicate. This was the sole writing system far advanced within a culture that was based on Stone Age times. Their unique script worked with over 1000 symbols or glyphs which represented either a word or distinct sillables. They also created codices (known by the name codices) made of paper made from bark of trees. They had a distinctive appearance, with the pages folding upwards, similar to the folding of an accordion. Furthermore they employed stones to carve their designs into, as well as bone. They also painted these intricate designs onto pottery.

What do these Mayan texts depict?

The writings that were written by the Mayan people included astronomy, divination, and religious rituals of a nature. They also provide us with an abundance of information regarding the Maya. Actually, they are the basis of the most significant historical significance in this regard. In the earlier part of this book, many of the texts were destroyed or burned during the time of Spanish invaders due to the content being viewed as sinful and pagan. But, there are three codices (books) that were able to survive the scourge. They were designated Paris, Madrid, and Dresden following the cities which contain these codices. This Codex of Dresden has within it extremely specific tables for the moon and Venus and also goes into details on how to anticipate solar eclipses.

Mayan Texts later translated:

Other crucially important texts created by educated Indians who could summarize and translate the records of Mayan hieroglyphs to scripts of their own Latin language. The texts that were translated include chronicles of the prophecies, divination and myths. Another text includes medical information and other images of a spiritual nature. The most well-known of all texts translated was written in the Mayan language known as Quiche which was later translated into it's Spanish language. The translation was done by a priest and the text was full of information on cosmology and mythological details about the Maya in modern-day Guatemala.

Influences are the most prominent that have influenced the history from central Mexico. In the same book the chronicles describe the creation of man as well as the specific actions of godly characters, as well as the people from the Quiche period, and their monarchs. These specific fragments of writing from the time that belonged to the Mayan people were not considered to be authoritative or sacred in their own right (like those of the Quran as well as the Bible) however, they were regarded as records of rituals, knowledge, and practices.

More details on the Astronomy and writing habits that are characteristic of Ancient Maya:

Record keeping was essential to the Mayan people and was essential for astronomy, prophecies and agricultural activities. It was important to keep this data was vital to know when the seasons would be wet or dry, which allowed Mayans to know when it was the ideal time to plant and harvest their crops. Additionally they also recorded the motions of celestial bodies (like the planets, stars moon, sun, and stars) which allowed them to create calendars that were accurate that can be utilized to predict the future. purposes.

Record keeping on a regular basis enabled people of the Mayan people to accurately forecast the cycles of planets and those of Venus eclipses, Venus, and moon. This helped in determining the dates when the planet's bodies would be in the most suitable locations for undertaking activities such as pursuing battles, trading expeditions or the inauguration of the kings and other ceremonies that were held. This data served as a reference point for numerous significant events that were important to those of the Mayan people.

Retrospectively looking at these Records in the present day:

There was a text from the ancient times from the Maya that even recorded the precise moment that an astronomer of a royal standing made a breakthrough discovery about Venus traveling across the sky at night. The text provided precise measurements of the patterns Venus created when she was rising and setting. These precise recordings permit historians to pinpoint precisely when the astronomer was alive, which was just the quarter century in the 10th century. In this document you can see exactly when the scientist had his ground shaking realizations.

The fascinating History of the Codex of Dresden:

It is a Codex is a document from the Mayan time, comprising 39 pages, each one written on a double-sided. The Codex is fascinating and tangled background. The text somehow made its way through into the Peninsula of

Yucatan to the point of getting to Germany during the late 1700s. A century later, an academic from Germany who had no prior knowledge about the history or culture of the Mayan people was perusing this codex. He came across a page of numbers and was able to discern the table contained details concerning the solar system Venus. It happened even the fact that there was no person during that time that could discern the mysterious symbols.

Another time, around a century later, in the early 1800s, an engineer looked over the data carefully and came to the conclusion that Mayan people were using an elaborate method of making the most of a shift to their celebrated calendar. The reason for this change was Venus who was operating an irregular cycle in the time. Many people had thought that they were able to achieve these corrections by using methods of a numerological kind like creating the events of Venus in the past and then predicting the movement of the future based on this calculation.

Looking more closely at the text that is surrounded by the Table:

However, few people took the time to look at the written language in the context of the numbers on that table. This wasn't the fault of the people who looked at it since we were not capable of deciphering the symbols yet and would not be able to until some time later. When we looked at the text around the tables for Venus found in the document it was discovered that the prehistoric Mayans had the ability to precisely calculate Venus phases. This enabled them to plan ceremonies and events more precisely. The event that was believed to be a fictitious occasion involving Venus turned out to be a valid estimation of the planet's shifting.

Rituals concerning The Shifts of Venus:

The Mayan people are famous for their rituals that were intricate and closely tied in their calendar. It is probable from the data in the translated text that they were carrying out rituals of a massive scale that were tied in some way to Venus and the various phases the planet experienced. This is why the changes were included in the chart of Venus. The reason was that they didn't want to observe their rituals at the wrong date. The smallest, insignificant information on their calendars don't appear important when viewed in a short-term perspective. But over the centuries inaccurate data could have resulted in significant mismatches between rituals intended to occur and when they occurred or didn't.

A Mysterious Mayan Astronomer:

The information contained in this document, in conjunction with the data on the table, indicates that the Maya used advanced techniques of scientific observation which indicates a specific time frame. This was probably around the decade of 10th century. A period of approximately 25 years was present in which this particular Mayan Astronomer was recording these observations. The Mayan person, whose name we don't know who they are, might be gazing at the night sky for a long time, and recording observation from the observatory.

The Evidence of the Hundreds of Years of Record Keepers:

This table matches another record of an event of Venus which was found in another ancient civilization called Maya. This was a civilization known as Copan and was located in present-day Honduras. The text was written two centuries prior to that of the Codex of Dresden suggesting that these people of the past were recording centuries-worth of information to be shared with future generations of people. The detail of these records amazing and precise, but the planning that went into these lengthy records is amazing and remarkable.

Venus is Even More Important to the Mayans. Mayans:

The information contained in the Codex from Dresden coincide with the time when Venus gained more importance in the people of Mayan religions. In the year around 300 A.D., up until 1000 A.D., also known as the Classic period, people in Tikal, Palenque, and Copan did not seem to be in any concern at all about the actions and changes of Venus. In the years following, however there was a new figure that appeared in the religious practices of the Maya which appeared to be a serpent sporting feathers (a very similar to

Quetzalcoatl the god worshipped by the Aztec the Aztec religion).

Chapter 5: The Mayan Calendar Mayan

Calendar

The Maya utilized a method of record of times that was very complex, and could be the most famous aspect or invention. This system is not in use today and was developed in complete isolation from other calendar systems that were used in earlier times. Unfortunately, this intricate calendar system came to an end when civilisation of Maya was destroyed. A large portion of the knowledge about the system was lost as the Spanish came in and took over.

What was the method by which this System utilized, and what is known about it?

Only in recent times in the 1990s to be precise archaeologists have discovered evidence that can help us comprehend these ancient people and their unique method of keeping track of dates and time. A method of writing that relies on symbols of a glyptic type was conceived and then created on buildings and artifacts that we have covered in detail in earlier chapters. The method was also painted onto the vases and then written on books (though there are a few today, as we was mentioned earlier).

Furthermore the Maya developed a method of keeping track of time, which included the concept of "long count". This technique was able to measure time with different units that ranged in duration, from one day, all the way to years of time that spanned millions (though this particular model was never employed). Contrary to what many people think, the system did not claim that the world was going to end in December 2012. The instrument that recorded million-year intervals of time provided enough proof for this. We'll go into more detail about the myth of 2012 later in this chapter.

It is the Vast Mathematical Knowledge of the Mayans:

They were extremely adept at maths and their knowledge is evident throughout this year's calendar. Along with being aware of and using the concept of zero, these individuals knew arithmetic on the level of modularity, mostly in the 20s. Yet, despite their ability to pay close attention to the sky and planets however, their calendar, shockingly is not a direct reflection of the lunar cycles as well as the seasonal changes. The calendar isn't even aligned with the years according to the cycles of sun. It's not like the Mayan people weren't aware of this but they didn't have any desire or need to sync their calendars to the solar cycle, as other civilizations in earlier times in the Old World once did.

the Three Types of Calendars that the Mayans employed:

There was not just one type of calendar that was used by the Mayans There were three distinct kinds:

*The Long Count Calendar: This type of calendar was used primarily to record historical events due to its capacity to determine dates that are millennia apart, either of the past or future.

*The Tzolkin Calendar was solely used to be used for ceremonies and comprised of 13 days and 20 of these 13 day intervals. This calendar would cycle through the close of the cycle every there were 260 days in the calendar. We don't know what makes this cycle significant but it is possible that it is linked to Venus the orbit of Venus that covers a span which is 263 consecutive days.

*The Haab Calendar: This type was a model for civil use that utilized the idea of a year with 360 days, that had 20 days in each period. There were 18 times. At the end of each year the year, there would be five additional days to try and ensure that it was in sync with the sun's cycle.

The dates of calendars Tzolkin and Haab calendars did not have the same year-long component However, the combination of dates from both calendars can indicate a day that is near within a 52-year cycle. years.

Myths regarding what is known about the Long Count Calendar of the Mayans:

There was no particular date of departure for any calendar used by the Mayan inhabitants, and they seemed to have viewed the concept of time as infinity, not having a end nor beginning. Many erroneous theories were created using the long-count method used by people of the Mayan people. The belief was that the calendar would be able to end at some point and that there could be an Apocalypse or a shift in the poles, the convergence of the universe or a massive shift in the world. Because of the design of the long-term calendar and its reliance on cycles and cycles, this is a hurriedly leap to the conclusion, to at the very least. This is what caused many people to falsely be afraid of 2012.

The Cycle of Mayan people's beliefs:

When a cycle ends it triggers the start of a new cycle. This happens throughout the year in the words of the Mayans. Therefore, the date of 21st December 2012 had nothing to do with the 1999's December! Because it is the case that the Mayan calendar isn't utilized for as long, any theories about trying to figure out the "end of the era" by using it is just speculation, nothing more. The height in the Mayan civilization has been debated for decades and years. The date we are currently assuming is based on methods of science such as carbon dating however, we might be wrong by a few years. Therefore, any theories regarding the prediction of the future using this old calendar are likely to be incorrect.

Untruths about 2012 and why they were false:

The same could be said regarding the age of Christianity that may likely be just in the next few years. That means that all forecasts concerning the end of the world were nonsense and unattainable. Furthermore is the notion that an event occurring in the millennium that is was based on Christian time-recording techniques would indicate the end of the world is based on math that is based on base 10 and the Mayans employed 20s. This is yet another example of that it's impossible to draw any conclusions from the calendar used by those of the Mayan people. Furthermore, 2012 is gone, but the earth remains.

The entire doomsday forecast for 2012 was a complete misunderstanding in its earliest stages and right from the beginning. The calendar, in contrast to the self-proclaimed prophets of the coming end of time, did not end in 2012 and there was no prophecy which claimed that the end of the world would occur on the 21st of December of the year. Yet, rumors ran everywhere and people were frightened. But the truth behind the myth might be much more fascinating. A logical-minded scientist by the name of Carlson who studied galaxies far away as a profession, initially was interested in this doomsday prediction in the 1970s, at a conference on the Mayan civilization.

The Amazing Grasp the Mayans were able to use of Time:

In the area where Mesoamerican rainforests still exist it was once home to an incredible civilization. As we now know were able to construct amazing pyramids, massive temples, as well as bustling, complex cities. At its peak around 800-800 A.D., citizens heavily were residing in the area. in urban areas, they had nearly two thousand people for each square mile. A modern-day equivalent of this is L.A. The people who lived there mastered a complicated dialect, and left astonishing clues regarding their day to daily lives, and were experts in the field of astrology as we discussed in the past.

However, of all these fascinating facts regarding the Mayan people one of the most fascinating of all was their astonishing ability to comprehend time. The length of time they recorded or project far exceed the modern technology in terms of length and length. From our current knowledge, we are able to estimate that the Big Bang happened in between 13 and 14 billion years ago. Many time and date references found in the ruins of the Maya date back not just millions and billions of years more than the Big Bang date. The method of keeping a calendar, was referred to as the long count was designed specifically for longer durations of time and is the most complex system of timekeeping that has ever been used.

How does the Long Count Calendar Functions:

The calendar is written using contemporary typography that resembles the odometer inside your car. It is a base-20 which is modified and features moving numbers that represent 20-day intervals. Since the numbers rotate the calendar allows it to "roll" and then start again. This repetition of numbers is the primary reason behind confusion over 2012. What is the reason for the Maya decline? One archaeologist has a theory that was formulated by analyzing the data of NASA.

Bak'tuns- One Mayan Unit for Measuring Time:

In the religion of the Mayan people, it is stated that our world was created five hundred and fifty-one years earlier. This is the date that we call today "the year" 3114 B.C. In the event of this it would have been displayed as a 13 and after that, four zeros. On the 21st of December, 2012, it appeared exactly the same, the 13 with four zeros. According to researchers studying the Maya there were 13 Bak'tuns between these two dates which is 13 times that lasted 144,000 consecutive days. According to the religion of the Mayan people, this span of time was important, but not as many believed, a sign of imminent destruction. There aren't any tablets or ruins or stones that remain in the ruins that predict the end of the world to its end.

No anomalies to support theories of Doomsday Theories:

Modern scientists are in agreement with this. Experts from NASA recently met to discuss what they discovered. The meeting concluded the absence of comets nor asteroids headed towards the earth that were discovered. There was no planet heading towards us to destroy us and, if it was, it would've been visible through the night sky. To verify this, all one has to do is to go outside and look upwards. The sun was not at risk in 2012 either. It was exploding for years from the time Mayan people were able to observe it and it never destroyed our planet. At the moment the sun was heading to its highest level in a period of 11 years of activity, which means that it was comparatively less powerful than the preceding five decades. Reports that said the opposite was false.

What would Maya have viewed Our "End of the Earth" Frenzies?

What would the people of ancient times who invented this remarkable calendar tell us about this? If they were able to, somehow, recognize that the month of 2012's December was nearing and they could have remarked that the date was significant. Many believed that their gods created the world more than five thousand years ago and that they were returning. One particular god was believed by a few to be returning to restore order to the fabric of space and time, and to rejuvenate the universe. Also, if the prophecy was saying something, it was that the world would be rejuvenated and rejuvenated, not washed out, destroyed or destroyed. Humans have predicted their own demise for a long time, from before the age, and the 2012 plot was only the latest frenzied.

Chapter 6: Gods And Religion

The Mayan people developed a complex culture that was from the other cultures of the time, even before Spaniards arrived in the region. The Mayan religion Maya concentrated on the worship of Gods associated with nature (particularly the god of corn rain god as well as the sun god). The religion also comprised an elite group of priestly citizens who were devoted to Astrology and astronomy, as well with the building of pyramid temples. We'll discuss this in the previous chapter. Certain of the practices that the Maya took part in for their reasons of religion was extremely violent and to us, cruel however we will leave this for the final chapter.

The Remaining Remnants of Mayan Religion in Modern Day:

As we discussed earlier, when the Spanish came to the Kingdom of the Maya, they erased a significant part of the texts that were related to their faith, going as far as to torch books. Because of this, it's difficult to determine what the religion was about, or even to follow with it fully. There are however, certain aspects of the Maya religion Maya that are still in use today times, along in people of Indians from Maya origin who reside within Central America and Mexico. These people follow a mix with Roman Catholicism and also their traditional faith. The Maya's religion Maya was extensively discussed as the time got towards 2012.

This is the Creation Myth of the Mayan World:
Mayan People had a complex and lengthy story of their mythological origins which was told by one of their remaining sacred texts. In these myths gods that were the forefathers of Maya created the earth from a gap of water, and blessed the earth with animals and plants. The creation of sentient beings was not easy however, eventually humans were created. There was among these humans the famous twin heroes who embarked on a variety of adventures that included their battle with the lords of the underworld. Their tale reached the point when their god, the corn god (their dad) was revived. This is a clear indication that

the whole cycle of mythology here was a reference to the fertileness of maize.

This is the universe of Mayan People:

The most cherished belief held by Maya's time was that Maya was that all matter or objects in the universe had distinct levels or degrees of holy qualities and strength. That is they considered everything sacred in a certain sense that was not limited to a few objects. Their concept of the universe was the space which the Maya resided in (the Earth), the invisible realm that the celestial gods resided in (the sky) and the invisibly realm of the water which was inhabited by gods from the underworld.

The Mayan God of Creation:

There were many gods that were considered to be of important positions in the Mayan people. Each one of them had both a positive and negative aspect to them. However, the most important was known as Itzamnaaj (also known as Itzamna in various translations). The god who created it was and the ruler of all forces that exist in the universe and naturally fight one another: sky and earth night and day death and life. This god, who was god of the celestial realm was portrayed as being the Milky Way, but was also depicted as a reptile with two heads or at times as the serpent. The figure was often called god of fire.

Deities who the Maya held dear:

Alongside the God of Creation in Maya, there are many other significant figures from the Maya religion that you should know about. Other significant gods included:

"The god of lightning known as K'awlil. He was depicted with an upside-down snout and a snake's foot and a protruding object out of his face. This object was often depicted as an axe or tube or a pipe, or a pipe, and was smoking.

* God who is responsible for thunderstorms also known as Chaak. The god of clouds struck to bring thunder and rain and thunder, and was known as Tlaloc by people of the Aztec people. Although certain Mayan farmers believed in one god of rain while others believed that an entire order of gods associated with rain existed. In other myths, gods of rain attack snakes who carry rain using their axes.

* The sun god is known as K'inich Ajaw. In the mythology of the Quiche Mayans the god who made light and the days. He was also known as the sun's face and was a popular god of healing and medicine.

Also, there was Kukulcan (though several translations and spellings exist) The god appeared as a serpent sporting feathers. He was also seen on a variety of Mayan temples. The god later became popular with those of Aztecs along with the Toltec people and was renamed to Quetzalcoatl.

* One of the gods mentioned above included Bolon Tzacab, who was often depicted having a nose with branches and is by the ruler, resembling the Scepter. The god is believed by many to have been the god of blood royal or descent.

Beliefs regarding Death as well as the Afterlife:

Caves are important to the religion of the Mayans because it was believed that they served as entrances into the underworld. Caves were holy and dangerous places where people who died were buried and where rituals for the ancestors were conducted. What the Mayan beliefs about the afterlife was a risky journey of the deceased's soul through the realm of gods who were evil. The journey was made in the dark and deep underworld, and was represented by the jaguar (or night symbol in the case of those who were Mayans). The majority of Mayan people, including King, ended in the underworld. Only those who passed away in childbirth or committed suicide, were killed fighting for their lives, or been sacrificed may be taken directly to heaven.

Rituals to commemorate death:

Funeral rituals were an essential part of the religious beliefs of the Maya and they revered the process of dying greatly. In their society death was a thing to be fearful of and those who died were to be grieved deeply. They also believed that certain deaths were more significant in comparison to other death. They heavily relied on rituals, and placed a great importance on them. They made sure to pay high respect to the character of destruction portrayed through their Gods. This meant they made certain to honor those who had died with the help of traditions and honored ancestors that were long dead.

Burial Customs for Maya Deceased Maya:

Mayans who died had their bodies buried in corn placed into their mouths. We know that the Mayans put a lot of importance on corn in their religion and believed that it was a symbol of resurrection and was believed to provide food for the dead on their journey into other realms. Furthermore they also put stones or jade beads inside the mouth of the deceased, to ensure that they had funds to pay for their journey. Sometimes, whistles made to look like gods or animals or gods, and made of stone, were placed in the offerings to the tomb, with the hope of helping the deceased go to the other side of the world.

The Color Red The Color Red Graves as entrances:

The color red for the Mayans was significant as it represented rebirth and death. Because of this, they frequently used Cinnabar to cover the graves and skeletons of the deceased. The deceased bodies were typically wrapped in cotton mantles prior to burials. The burial sites were meant to offer access to realms far above this world. Each one of the graces would face east or north, with a view towards Maya's heavens. Maya While other graves were placed in the manner mentioned earlier in the chapter, inside caves to offer access into an entrance into the Mayan underworld.

The rituals and practices of death among the Mayan people evolved as the years progressed and we can discern this through archaeological evidence and artifacts from various period. After the time of the late period, also called the Preclassic was established, the dead were laid to rest in their graves in a flexed and slouching posture. The deceased were laid to rest where their bodies were extended. In the later years, top and most elite members constructed tombs that were vaulted while other rulers demanded the construction of huge burial structures. were built. Then, just cremating the dead became the standard procedure.

What is the reason behind The Common Afterlife Idea?

It isn't possible to say with certainty if there was an idea of an afterlife that was customary prior to the Spanish conquered Mayan territory. It is believed that the Maya of Yucatec origin believed there were multiple paths could be taken after you passed away. A tomb that was discovered that contained a pot within it was a representation of the family members of the kings of Mayan times, rising from the ground , like trees, and creating an area of trees. There were several types of ancestral worship among the Mayans and included the construction of idols that contained the remains of cremation of the dead. They also provided food to the graves of the deceased during occasions of celebration and sometimes temples were built over an urn containing cremated remains.

the Rulers of Maya Are they semi-divine Beings?

Rulers from Mayan days were said to be intermediaries between the citizens as well as holy gods. They were believed to be divine, in addition. They were believed to communicate with Gods through ways no normal citizen could. In the end, the rulers were laid to rest in elaborate tombs that were filled with gifts of high significance.

Maybe these were intended as gifts to the gods, or just offerings to the rulers who died.

There is no distinction between religion and Science:

Contrary to other societies in the past, the Mayan people believed that science and religion were separate pursuits but they were the same. Therefore, they developed their intricate mathematical and astronomical systems and both were closely connected to religious ceremonies and rituals. Their math achievements comprised of having a notion of zero (very modern at the time) and also the use of positional notation. In their astronomy studies they were able calculate the duration of one cycle of sun's orbit with a high precision, and create chart of the positions of Venus and the moon and even forecast sun's eclipses and moon, in addition.

More details about this Mayan Beliefs of Time:

We discussed this topic in the chapter on calendars, however, the Mayans were able to demonstrate a solid and interesting understanding of time. They wanted to map and anticipate what would happen throughout the different cycles. This allowed them to gain the most they could from the natural processes of earth. The cosmological belief system they believed in stated that the planet was created and destroyed five times in various interpretations. Certain days throughout the year were considered as being reserved to specific actions, while others were considered to be bad or bad luck.

Mayan Divination Methods: Mayans:

They practiced divination which required their knowledge of astronomy and their complicated time-keeping system. The task of determining the days that were fortunate and not was the domain of priests, and also providing advice to kings about when was the most suitable time to begin a conflict, harvest crops or work on planting on the field. They were particularly fascinated by Venus and the sun. Venus and the movements of Venus. The ruling class of the Maya planned conflicts to coincide with the rising of Venus in the sky.

The Unlucky Day of Mayan Calendar: Mayan Calendar:

The calendar they utilized that we discussed in a previous chapter, was extremely complex and far more sophisticated than any calendar ever seen before or in the years since. The remarkable device featured an annual sun that was 365 days in length, and featured 20-day periods multiplied by 18 with a five-day period days which was thought to be extremely unlucky and negative. In keeping this period in mind and in mind, the Mayan people took all the measures necessary to guard themselves from the bad luck that they felt was approaching.

The Mayans Are a peaceful People?

From the beginning in the 90s scientists believed it was the case that Mayan people were peaceful peace-loving stargazers, who were concerned most of their religious beliefs and astronomical pursuits, but far from violence (unlike other civilizations nearby). The reason for this was their advanced knowledge of science that they displayed, their complicated society, and the texts scientists could translate their language from their time. However, over the years the majority of the hieroglyphics have been translatedand created an entirely different view for that of the Mayan people. The symbols suggest that the Maya rulers Maya began war against nearby cities, and took their kings captive and even beating the kings.

Chapter 7: What's The Reason For Their Decline?

To determine what was the reason that caused the Mayans to fall or, at the very least, abandon their cities to the west, we need to start by studying the causes of collapse for civilizations generally. The most common factor that causes the demise of strong natures, such as those of the Roman empire, is believed to be a mix of elements. Another feature similar to that which is evident in this instance is the disregard of rulers' resources, and the general welfare of the people they rule over. Are these features present during the time of Maya?

What was Things Like Right before the Collapse?

Prior to the Mayan collapse there were a few notable elements which could have played a role in the. They were conflicts that had no effect and extravagantly constructed structures, and the an over-exploitation of the forests, water and, in particular, the land. Historical historians of Mayan culture are able to settle on the primary contributing factors that may have contributed to this degeneration of the society. The main culprits are the result of overpopulation, drought and general war.

There are those who consider that the civilisation of Mayan people went extinct without a trace. However, this isn't the case. There are cities that, like Palenque, Copan, and Tikal were deserted just over 1000 years ago There are a number of plausible reasons to this, like conflict, climate change deforestation or drought. However, it is vital to keep in mind that the Maya weren't limited to a few regions as they were spread across many areas cities were growing while other cities slowed down or were abandoned. In reality Chichen Itza is the largest city in the world. Chichen Itza still has the largest ball court across all of the Americas.

Unsolved Mysteries and the future of Modern Maya:

The court is also bigger than a full length court for American football. The court's rings are believed that teams were trying to score on, somehow were 20 feet tall, more than twice the width that NBA baskets. It is the fact that people don't comprehend the rules of this game makes it even more difficult to comprehend. In earlier chapters of this book, the Spanish came to Mayan land and brought about major changes in the culture. They brought diseases that the Maya struggled with combating, and also burned their sacred texts, imposing Christianity on the Mayans. It is perhaps surprising that some (millions actually) Mayans survive today, in spite of the hardships they faced in the past.

Possible reasons for the collapse of the Mayan Empire:

Cities of the former Empire of the Mayans prospered and flourished in the northern regions of Central America and the south of Mexico for approximately six centuries. There is a belief that, around the year around 900 A.D., the civilization began to fall apart. Two new research projects that examine possible reasons why the civilization was destroyed, and they indicate the Mayan people as the primary culprits for the collapse of their empire.

* Deforestation and Drought Researchers have proven that drought is at the root of

the decline of the community. However it is the Mayan people appear to have made the problem more difficult by cutting off the trees that grew there to increase the harvest of crops and to build bigger cities. Researchers believe that the drought may have been caused by the forest destruction.

However, the removal of trees provides an reason to the dryness. It could, however, be able to explain the reason why the area seems to have dried out at that point. Simulations of climate conditions could give information about how changes in the forest and crop will affect the climate of this region. Results of this simulation indicated the cutting of as many trees can provide up to 60% of the drought that they endured. The switch to corn, rather than trees, will reduce the amount of the amount of water is absorbed by the atmosphere through the soil, thereby cutting in on rainfall.

Natural Environmental Changes: Another study revealed an alternative scenario, or maybe more complete. This suggests that the demise and devastation of the lowlands during the time was due to complicated interactions between the inhabitants who lived there and their surroundings. As we mentioned in the previous paragraph, it seems like cutting down the forest was a factor in the drought that seems to have reached its peak at the time the Maya population plummeted and then dramatically decreased.

However, this is just one part to the picture. The changing landscape could result in lower quality soil. There are other indications that the landscape was not in good condition like a deficiency of a certain kind of wood used for construction that was gone. There were also other species of animal, such as the deer breed, which appears to have drastically decreased when the empire came to an end.

Furthermore connections between social and economic relations might have played an important role in the demise in the Mayan civilization. Trade routes had changed from passages across the land to ships at sea. This shift could have made cities more vulnerable due to the change in their surrounding. With the pressures mounting and increasing in size, the ruling class (a small portion of the population) did not perform as they were supposed todeliver, creating more conflict. It is evident that the previous political and economic structure of partially divine rulers began degrading, causing artisans and peasants leaving their homes to pursue more lucrative opportunities elsewhere.

*War: As we talked on earlier the war was a normal element of the culture of the Maya for a number of years. But its size and intensity was increased prior to the collapse of their empire. This led cities to have to construct defensive forts. Prior to this, war had been commonplace, and losing typically meant a few important individuals being taken. As the years passed it appears that war has increased in severity and became increasingly damaging to all. The aim of capturing neighboring areas (in the hope of improving agricultural production) and committing a large amount of people as sacrifices (in the hope of pleasing gods for peace) became more important.

It is possible to look at archeological evidence which shows an increase in the number of arrows found in specific areas, indicating that life in cities was becoming more risky. Threats from the military could be involved also, however, evidence to support this is elusive. Many cities from this period can prove that destruction was deliberately caused by foreign troops.

* Overpopulation: Another possibility that has ascended upon the Maya and contributed to the production issues in the field of agriculture. The evidence from archeological excavations suggests that the cities of the region and the surrounding settlements were inhabited at a higher rate than they believed. More concerning, were the droughts that we mentioned earlier. However, not all Mayan city suffered from an extreme drought. It's evident that some lakes and rivers didn't dry out completely. In the regions that experienced an acute lack of drinking water, inability of agriculture and the absence of rain are enough to make it seem plausible that there was a rebellion among the inhabitants.

It could have been due to the common people (farmers) angered by the rulers, which led to residents leaving the area, or the social structure breaking down. There are some historical records that mention the events as the "descent" which suggests of a drastic decline in the number of people. However, there is no evidence of this massive shift in the population but there is a mention of the lowlands becoming totally abandoned after a collapse took place.

Many factors have contributed towards this Desertion of the Lowlands:

The previous paragraphs prove that there was no particular factor that led to the demise of the Maya and that it was the result of the environment. The social structure was in turmoil as well as war, climate problems and overpopulation all joined in a perfect order to destroy the existing order in the area. All of these elements could have been sufficient to be enough on their own but they were all arranged in in such the way that collapse was absolutely inevitable and the entire civilization was wiped out.

Thankfully, the fall of the classic Mayan people did not mean the end of the culture completely. While the Mayan culture suffered massive losses due to conflicts, war, destruction of forests, conflicts with the rulers, and also the arrival of the Spanish however, they're still in existence. There are people living today who continue to speak Mayan and some people who practice the religion carry even today. This is a testament to a remarkably robust group that had the capability to overcome any challenge and keep moving forward. As a result, they continue to carry on the legacy of this amazing tradition.

Chapter 8: What Happened To The Maya

Perform Human Sacrifice?

Researchers who study the Maya in the past believed that they were peaceful, and never was there a war among their own. The same scholars admired the scientific achievements and accomplishments of the ancient civilization and believed that violence couldn't be a part of this kind of knowledge and experience. However, more recent research revealed which questioned this and quickly proved it was the case that Mayans were tough and wary people who fought against one another frequently. As previously mentioned this constant conflict probably contributed to their elusive rapid loss of power, and we are certain that they were often involved in violent rituals.

Brutal Rituals performed by the Maya for religious reasons:

It's been said before, in this book that religion was extremely crucial to the Mayan lifestyle. Some of the practices they utilized to honor their religious beliefs were dramatic performances balls, games, prayers as well as competitions and dancing. It sounds like a simple thing however at the heart of these religious rituals was the idea of human sacrifice. It was believed that this practice would promote fertility, display the piety of the people and also to bless their gods. Also, it was believed Gods and goddesses from the Maya received nourishment from the blood of human beings which is why the practice of letting blood flow as a ritual was considered to be the main method of interaction with them. The Mayans believed that ignoring these rituals would cause chaos and severe disturbances in the universe.

The Process of Sacrificing:

At times of great importance that required sacrifice, the person to be sacrificed was put on an elevated structure (usually an elevated platform) or pyramid, while the priest cut their ribs right below and then removed the heart of the deceased by hand. Following this, the heart was burned because it was believed to feed the gods who were watching. Rituals from similar cultures also had rituals that resembled this, too. Maya believed in sacrifice and death.

Maya believed that death and sacrifice were tied in a spiritual manner to the notion of creation and rebirth generally. The same book describes the myth of creation of the Maya and the heroic twins' quests there is a tale of gods ask for human sacrifice, and then offers fire as a substitute.

A few hieroglyphics found in an excavation site suggests that the concept of beheading is connected conceptually, to the notion of creation or awakening, as per the Mayans. These sacrifices could also signal the beginning of new times that would usually mean the beginning of a brand new calendar cycle. The offerings made to gods were meant to assist in the renewal of the harvest of crops and also to help with the human cycles, and were considered essential to grow and survive. Sometimes, children could even be part of the victims.

Bloodletting to Royal Mayans:

It wasn't just vulnerable and unlucky victims who endured pain for gods for their sake. Nobles from the Mayan period were yet again, regarded as divine beings and royal blood was an important component in the ceremonies of the Maya and especially in the rituals that were related to agriculture. Indeed the elite people from Mayan communities, which were used as intermediaries between the people and gods, were subject to self-torture and bloodletting rituals for the sake of the religion. The more prominent one's status was, the more quantity of blood needed to be poured out.

It wasn't only males as well as female nobles had to go through this procedure. The process included the piercing of different organs, like the ears, tongue and lips, also known as the genitals with items like the spine of the Stingray. The remains of these spines are still found within ancient royal Mayan tombs. Blood sacrifices could be either dripped onto the paper, which would later be burned, or sprayed on idols of worship. The smoke that erupted due to the result was believed to open doors between realms or dimensions.

What were the occasions that Human Sacrifices were reserved for?

The sacrifice of the gods was a custom reserved on special occasions and was not meant to be an normal or commonplace practice. Maybe the Mayan people believed that making it an everyday event of life would diminish the significance of the ritual however the specifics of this are not clear and we are only able to speculate. It was, in lieu of being a common practice, it was necessary (in the view that of Mayan people) to honor specific rituals like the inauguration of a ruler or a new heir chosen to the throne. Furthermore it was possible for a sacrifice to be used to honor the opening of a temple or ball court. The victims of these rituals were prisoners of war.

The Relationship of this Practice with Mayan Ball Game: Mayan Ball Game:

For Mayan people sacrifices were usually linked to the game they played on ball courts. The game, which involved balls made of rubber that was thrown across the court by the hips of players. The game often carried an underlying spiritual or symbolic significance. Images from Mayan culture show a significant connection to decapitated heads as well as the balls, which were sometimes, made of skulls of humans. The ball games would often be a continuation of the battle which was won. This could mean, it is believed that warriors who were taken from tribes or states of war had to participate in the game and be sacrificed following the game.

In Chichen Itza, the city Chichen Itza, the unfortunate victims who were sacrificed were covered with blue paint. This hue could be in honor of Chaak, the most revered and well-known Mayan god. Then, they would be dropped into a nearby water source. Furthermore close to the ball court on Chichen Itza's site Chichen Itza, a panel depicts a vivid image of a sacrifice of a person taking place. It is believed to is a picture of one of the players who were sacrificed from either the winning team or the losing team when the game had come to an end.

Beheading and Disemboweling:

To the north of this area, the tribes of the Aztecs ruled, who be infamous for their similar procedure to remove the heart, which included offering an organ (often still beating) to gods higher up. As we've mentioned earlier, Mayan people also removed the hearts of their victims, that is evident in representations found at historic places, like Piedras Negras, but it is evident that it was more typical to disembowel or even decapitate their victims. Another method of sacrificing was simply shoving the tied-up victim into the stones of the huge temples.

Different methods for different victims:

The method used for each victim depended on the individual and the reason they were being sacrificed. The different victims were dealt different fates, however each was equally terrible. For instance, those who were seized as prisoners of war faced the unfortunate experience of being disembowelled. In the case of human sacrifices that were related to the game of football it is likely that victims will be taken into the ground or even decapitated. Most often, these methods of killing were combined together to create another kind of.

How is Human Sacrifice connected to Politics:

King and rulers who were captives were regarded as the most highly valued human sacrifices. At times, prisoners was sacrificed when forced down the steps as well as playing on the court. It appears that nobody within the Mayan society was immune to this brutal, yet in the time, normal routine. The historical evidence of these stories shows that no matter how advanced or sophisticated human beings have become, violence was a common feature of societies. Did this approach to life an element in the reason the Maya was destroyed? Perhaps we'll never know.

Chapter 9: The Early Settlers

Pre-classic Period, c. 2000 B.C. until 250 A.D. Before you embark on to explore the story of Mayan Civilization, let us begin by discussing a few points. The first would be an understanding of Maya. Maya is also called Mayan is the American Indian people who lived in Belize, Guatemala, and Yucatan. The remarkable tradition of the Mayans especially the pottery they used, their astronomy and architecture and writing system was at its peak between 300 to around 900 A.D.

Mayans should not mix with Aztecs and the Incans and the Olmecs as each of their cultures is distinct in their own ways. The Mayans were the first to arrive in Mesoamerica and were the ones who endured the longest and were considered by historians to be the most important. As they began to build villages throughout the area and were later followed by the Olmecs the Inca along with the Aztecs. Learn more about Mayans and their neighbors in the chapters to follow. Mayans as well as their neighbours in subsequent chapters.

You are set to embark on an adventure that takes you back a few thousand years back to witness the creation of a civilization that was once thriving. Find out the ways in which the Mayans developed from a tiny village network to an enormous city in the midst of the lowlands of the tropical rainforests of Mesoamerica.

At one point that was more than two thousand years prior to the Christian period, an ancient group of people had started building settlements on old lowlands that were located in the Pacific coast's

Soconusco region. This region was ideal for farming since there were hardly any hills. Thus, the early Mayans cultivated their primary food consisting of squash, maize chili peppers, cassava and beans. At the same time they also worked by making pottery made of clay and figurines.

As time passed, these roots settlements developed into larger cities. One of them was Nakbe, a city. Nakbe in the north of Africa. It was here that the early Mayans extracted the limestones they used to construct a number of their temples. Nakbe as well as the other cities were linked by thesacbe (which means "white roads") an interconnected causeway which was typically constructed thirteen feet above ground level and was covered with finely crushed white stones.

A city that thesacbeled to was the dazzling El Mirador. El Mirador. Despite the harsh, barren , tropical soil upon which the city was constructed the ancient inhabitants were savvy enough to to create a system of agriculture. What they did was carried thousands of kilograms of the mud of the swamps that were seasonal in the region and then mixed it into lime to form terraces suitable for the planting of. El Mirador also became the location of three famous top pyramids. One of them is 180 feet tall and referred to by locals today asEl Tigre. The other, regarded to be one of the largest pyramids in the world, is La Danta, which is estimated as being 236 feet high. The third, and the least knownis the Los Monos.

A city in the highlandsof Kaminaljuyu also grew to the point where historians believe that it is the first example of the most complex social and cultural system of Mesoamerica. It was a hub for trade between Maya lowlands as well as those of the Pacific coast. Avocados, maize, cotton cacao, cocoa, palm nuts black plums, and beans were among the agricultural products that were grown in the region. According to some, the economic activity at Kaminaljuyu was so large that people were forced to throw away large quantities of garbage.

At this point the people started to establish themselves in Mesoamerica too They were also referred to as"the Olmecs according to the Aztecs. Olmec is originated from two

Aztec words: olli, which means "rubber," andmecatl, or "people."

The Olmecs were the founder patrons of ritualistic practices such as bloodletting for religious purposes and the dangerous Mesoamerican ball game. They are also credited with designing"colossal heads," also known as "colossal head," they are 17 to more massive stone sculptures thought to be the representation of the Olmec rulers.

A large portion of Mesoamerican culture - and that includes the of the Mayans was inspired by the Olmecs who settled in 1400 B.C. Their existence lasted around 1,000 years and, throughout their time they were able to expand their culture quite remarkable, particularly in regards to mathematics, art as well as astronomy and agriculture.

Mayan intellectual and artistic development continued to increase throughout the Pre-classic Period. Around 700 B.C., they began to develop their famous writing system. Later around the year 400 B.C., they started carving their first calendars from stone.

Around the year 100 B.C., they began making their first pyramids.

The same was true of the cities of the Preclassic Mayan civilization. But, by the beginning of the 1st century A.D., many of these cities fell into disuse. The causes of this demise remain a mystery. The historians can only speculate that causes like extreme environmental changes caused the land to be not suitable for farming and, consequently, inhabited.

Chapter 10: Golden Age Of Monuments

Classic Period, c. 25o to around 900 A.D.

Between 250-900 A.D., Mayan civilization in the lowlands continued to evolve into larger cities, greater monuments and more fine artworks. Every city functioned as an urban-state, meaning that a large city was the central point for the regions surrounding it, which included farms and trade routes. Within each city , there was an incredibly grand palace in which the king of the city resided.

Of the 40 of the Mayan cities Six are the most popular. These include El Mirador, Kaminaljuyu, Tikal, Caracol, Chichen Itza and Teotihuacan.

In the preceding Chapter, El Mirador was one of the longest-running and most populous cities-states. There was a period in the past when it was the home of over 100 thousand people which is a staggering amount in comparison to neighboring cities. The residents had left the city before the beginning in the Classic Period (that is, prior to the year 150 A.D.), they returned around 700 A.D.

Within the Guatemala mountains was the state-of-the-city of Kaminaljuyu. It was known as a significant center of commerce and trade, specifically with regard to cacao, obsidian fruit and pottery. Mayans resided in the city from 1200 B.C. between 1200 B.C. and around 900 A.D.

City-states like Tikal is among the most well-known of the city-states that have been established in Mayan time. It is the home of many landmarks, including Tikal's Temple IV. In the present, Tikal, together with the Chicken Itza are designated by the UNESCO as UNESCO World Heritage sites.

Caracol is situated in what is now referred to as the Cayo district in Belize began as an independent state that was a client of Tikal after Tikal was granted power. But it was separated from Tikal about the year 600 A.D. and gained its independence, even achieving an estimated population of 180,000, and covering more than 200 square kilometers.

At the close of Classic period in the late Classic period, it was the city state in Chichen Itza that became the most strong. The various monuments built within the city included The Great Ball Court, the El Castillo pyramid, and the Temple of the Warriors. In the Great Ball Court was known as being five hundred feet and 230 feet and had walls that reached up to 26 feet tall. El Castillo was originally built as a temple for worship of Kukulkan and stood taller than 98 feet. Its Temple of the Warriors was another massive pyramid in the form of a huge temple that was built on top of four platforms, and covered with 200 columns.

Although Chichen Itza was the biggest city-state at the time in the Classic Period, this title should have been given over to Teotihuacan metropolis that was established at the beginning of the present. Teotihuacan was regarded as the most populous city within the New World, triggered the beginning of the rapid growth that was the Mayan civilization. Although Teotihuacan was not a strictly Mayan state, the city was so dominant during the period that it greatly influenced Mayan culture.

In actual fact the year the year 378 A.D., Teotihuacan managed to take on nearby cities like Tikal and overthrow their monarchs to create a new dynasty which was connected to it. The Mayan warlord who commanded this battle was SiyajK'ak' (whose name means Fire is Born). The king Chak Tok Ich'aak I of Tikal died in the same year Siyaj K'ak' arrived in Tikal in which case it could be that the battle was bloody.

The year the year 379 A.D., Siyaj K'ak was in charge of the beginning of the new Dynasty of Tikal. Yax Nuun Ahiin I was to become the new king. his power as a politician was the reason that led Tikal into becoming the world's most powerful town within the Mesoamerican lowlands.

Tikal wasn't the sole city-state that was powerful in the world at the time. Its main adversary was the town-state of Calakmul situated located in Calakmul, which was located in the Peten Basin. Both of these cities had established allies and vassals in smaller cities that were used to try to take over each other.

The year the year 629 A.D., in an attempt to extend the rule of Tikal beyond the boundaries of B'alaj Chan K'awiil, prince of the King of Mwaan Jol II, traveled in 629 A.D. to Dos Pilas I in the Petexbatun region to build an entirely new city. For the next twenty years, B'alaj Khan K'awiil was the ruler of Dos Pilas and fought alongside Tikal in the battle against Calakmul. In 648, his capture was by the King of Calakmul Yuknoom Ch'een II. It is known that he later restored as the ruler of Dos Pilas, however at this point, he had become an all-weather ally of Calakmul.

At the time of the year 426 A.D., another city-state developed within the southwest. It was called the Copan city. Copan and was founded by King K'inich Yax Mo' who was allied with Teotihuacan as well as Tikal. Between the years 695-738 A.D., Copan reached its peak of culture under the rule of Uaxaclajuun Ub'aah K'awiil. However, he was later captured from the army of Quirigua ruler K'ak'Tiliw Chan Yopaat and perhaps with the assistance of Calakmul. The king was later executed in Quirigua and this led to the demise of the once-powerful city-state.

The end the Classic Period, in 9th century A.D., the Mayan people began moving north and leave behind their magnificent cities. In 900 A.D., in particular this was the year that Teotihuacan became abandoned signalling the closing of the Classic Period. It is likely that war or drought as well as overpopulation were some of the major factors that led to this decline.

Chapter 11: The Maya Highlands

Post-Classic period, c. 995 until 1539 A.D.

Following the departure of large city-states of during the Classic Period, the Mayans began to settle in regions that bordered more permanent water sources. Yet, conflict continued to be a problem for the various cities in this Post-Classic Period. Many of the cities were built on tops of hills and were surrounded by deep ravines that reduced their vulnerability to attack. Many even have ditches or walls around them to provide additional defense.

Chichen Itza became recognized as the most powerful city-state in Chichen Itza's glory in 925 A.D., and this continued for about 200 years. It was not up to the year 1250 A.D., according to the historical records, that residents left it.

From the year 1283 A.D., the city-state of Mayapan was declared the capital city for Mayapan, the capital of Mayan civilization. It was a time of growth with the establishment of new cities as well as trade networks across the Caribbean and Gulf coasts. According to the legend the city was founded in the name of Mayan god Kukulcan after the demise of Chichen Itza. The god was the one who spoke to the regional lords to resolve their differences and to join in one central city, Mayapan, whose name means "Standard for Maya People." Maya People."

The leader of the Cocom family, a rich and long-standing bloodline, was elected as the king of Mayapan. The noble families as well as lords of cities surrounding were summoned to take on government roles, and possibly take on the role of hostages to secure their families' support. The capital was overseen by an assembly which included God's king as well as Shaman in the top post.

In the year 1448 A.D., Mayapan was abandoned by its people due to a rebellion. According to some, continuous political and social turmoil as well as environmental changes that led to the deportation.

Following the time that the Mayans left Mayapan in the late 19th century, the Yucatan peninsula was stricken by numerous conflicts, plagues and environmental catastrophes. In spite of the absence of a capital city-state within the region, there were numerous Mayan cities remained thriving in their economics were related. They shared a common cultural tradition, however there was a wide range of differences regarding the political and social structure. The Ki'che' , in particular could build an empire of a few hundred people that ruled large portions in the highlands west of Guatemala and also the surrounding Pacific coast.

Another capital city of the state was Q'umarkaj that translates to "the location of the decayed cane" or "the site of the old Reeds." The capital was a part to the fierce K'iche kingdom. The city, fortified, was located on the highlands in Guatemala and was administered by King K'iq'ab. Some of the more notable structures in Capital was the temple dedicated to Tohil Jaguar, the patron saint of the city as well as it was also the home of Jakawitz the god of the mountains. Another temple was that of Awilix god of the noble family. another temple was that of Q'uq'umatz. Feather Serpent god, who was also the person who established the city.

Q'umarkaj was among the strongest and most recent Mayan cities when Spanish conquistadors arrived in 16th century. The remaining lords from the K'iche' Maya invited Spanish conquistador Pedro de Alvarado in March 1524. The latter had was able to defeat the K'iche's army in Quetzaltenango valley, and whose troops defeated one of four Lords from Q'umarkaj, namely Tecun Uman. Alvarado was suspicious it was an omen or scam and therefore the forces he led camped on the outskirts of the city and instead invited the Oxib-Keh and Beleheb Tzy, two of the most powerful lords of this city to visit instead. After they arrived the latter, he kept the two as prisoners.

The K'iche's warriors to assault the indigenous allies of Spanish conquistadors. After the warriors were able to eliminate the one Spanish soldier Alvarado later decided to take two of his hostages and burn them to death. Following that, he burned the whole capital.

Chapter 12: The Spanish Conquest

Contact Time, 1511-1697 A.D.

It was 1511 that the Spanish first reached the shores of Yucatan. It was an accident landing, as their boat was destroyed within the Caribbean. In 1517, when the Maya warriors took on the Spanish majority of them were executed, but two managed to escape free. Between 1517 and 1519 more Spanish conquistadors started to enter Mayan areas and fighting locals.

In 1521 In 1521, in 1521, the Spanish conqueror Hernan Cortes was invited into the Aztec capital city of Tenochtitlan. Evidently, the king as well as his court mistook him for be the god of prophecy of the East. In the end it was the time that the Spanish were successful in taking over the capital. Cortes named a man Pedro de Alvarado y Contreras to Guatemala and a huge Spanish army. They reached their destination in 1523 , and within the year, they defeated Q'umarkaj, the capital of the city state. Q'umarkaj.

In a brief period during which the Spanish were allies with Iximche, the Mayan capital of Iximche however, later Iximche's citizens were forced to flee due to their inability to surrender to their Spanish conquistadors' irrational demands for gold as a tribute from them.

In 1525 in 1525, Zaculeu, Mam Mayan capital city Zaculeu was destroyed by Spanish soldiers, which caused its inhabitants to flee their homes too. The Mayans took sanctuary in Xinabahul and, however, in 1525, this temporary shelter was destroyed by the Spanish who were led by Gonzalo de Alvarado and Contreras, twin brother of Pedro de Alvarado. In 1525 that followed, the Mam Maya was forced to surrender.

Each day at a time, the Mayan cities of the Yucatan Peninsula fell as the Spanish conquistadors attacked one after the next. By 1546, Spanish had been able to completely conquer the northern region of the peninsula. This means that the remaining Mayan kingdoms were situated in the Peten basin as well as Nojpeten as their capital city. Nojpeten as their capital city.

In 1697, more than 200 Spanish soldiers and more than 100 native laborers, led by

Martin de Ursua y Arismendi reached the western shores of the Lake of Peten Itza. With an attack boat they brutally killed a large number of Itza warriors and natives. After the attack the locals were compelled to leave Nojpeten. The city was then destroyed. big city in the Mayan Civilization.

Chapter 13: The Prest-Rulers

The Maya's government Maya was a mixture of civil and religious affairs. In reality the system was much similar to those of the Greek city-states. One man was in charge of cities or cities, as well as the rest of the area. The man was referred to as the halach the uinic, also known as "true one." It is pretty sure that both the ruler high priest were were the exact same individual. The halach the uinic only had to walk behind a tall Stela, a lavishly cut stone slab adorned with human figures and dates to alter his headdress and appear in the role of high priest.

The halach of uinic was adorned in brilliantly-coloured stunningly embroidered costumes and headdresses larger than him. According to the wall paintings discovered at Bonampak the earlobes of his were so big that earrings bigger than golf balls were able to be put inside the earlobes. The teeth of his were inlaid with jade. He had a bridge on his face that drew until mid-section of his sloping, flattened forehead. He was covered in tattoos. It is likely that he was also crossed-eyed. All in all, he must have been a spectacular appearance to the humble farmer.

High priests even if they weren't actually ruling, they were definitely councillors of the halach the uinic. They were thought-leaders, mathematicians, astronomers as well as astrologists and keepers of calendars. Their knowledge was carefully guarded and transferred through the generations from father to son or was taught in private only to priests' and nobles sons. They were also the supervisors of the public works, which produced the stunning temples and stone pyramids and many of them remain standing today.

The magnificently carved throne is located in Palace J-6 in Piedras Negras. According to hieroglyphic inscriptions, it was dedicated to God in A.D. 785

Below the level of civil and religious authority were numerous lesser priests and officials of the government. Certain priests were able to interpret the signs from the Gods within tiny villages, or presided on the altar of sacrifices. Other were medicinemen. Others were also guardians of the instruments that were played during funerals. The government employees were predominantly the local tax collectors as well as chiefs.

The Mayan civilization expanded and the priests of the aristocratic class increased in power. As time passed, the simple worship of the farmer's nature changed into something more complex. There were both good and evil gods, and at times one god could be equally positive and negative. Religion represented a constant struggle between gods. Only priests could read the signs and reveal the mysteries of death and life. They, the self-appointed god-interpreters were in charge of the lives of common farmers through a continuous religious circle. In the constant conflict of good and evil the farmers could not move without the permission of the priest. The day when an individual is born has been believed to determine the course of his life. The names of children were decided by priests. The time for planting corn was to be considered and confirmed by priests.

While Mayan religions were founded on the idea of magic, mystery and a little bit of hocus-pocus that was used to awe common Indians Many of them were inspired by the concept of the concept of time.

The concept of time, which refers to a series of ends and beginnings was an integral part of Mayan religion. The Mayans believed that time could reach back to darkness and the time of the beginning of the universe. The Maya believed this to be the date 4 Ahau 8 Cumhu that could be read as 3375 B.C., or 3111 B.C. Scholars disagree on this.

Time, following the completion of an extensive circuit, would return in the form of history. That is, it will repeat itself. The times that defined time such as the kin, uinal as well as tun and other were sacred. Every day was a god of the living and was known as "he," not "it." The gods of day carried the burden of the passage of time on their shoulders as they supported the weight of time with lines that ran across their shoulders and their foreheads. The gods of the gods are depicted in codices as well as on stelae. Every day god brought a prediction and some brought luck while others brought bad luck. Only a priest could calm the anger of the day-god.

A colorful wall painting is located inside the Temple of the Murals at Bonampak. The top painting depicts a high priest with his entire family members performing an act of bloodletting by puncturing their tongues. The painting below shows an elaborate dance performed on the steps of a pyramid.

A lot of Mayan writing dealt with the recording of time. The massive stone stelae as well as altars that are a part of so many palaces and temples, these steps, the walls and the panels, all carry dates symbols.

Through studying the movements of the moon and sun and planets such as Venus and Mars and the stars, priest-astronomers developed a calendar which was more accurate than other one in the world.

They had such a vast knowledge of astronomy, that the priests predicted moon eclipses precisely and accurately calculated they knew that Venus was a five-year year. A lot of their discoveries were likely based on the systems developed by the Olmecs, earlier people who lived near to each other.

The observatory located at Chichen Itza and the "sundial" at Copan were constructed to aid in research into astronomy like those at other locations. In many cities, like the one at Uaxactun (wah-shack Roox) as an example the building was constructed in order to show the longest and shortest days throughout the year. These observations were applied to practical, and religious application. Without this information what could priests instruct farmers on when to make their milpas and sow their fields?

Schematic of the Plaza of Group E, Uaxacten, Peten. By taking specific sights of Pyramid E-7, the Mayan priest-astronomers were able determine the length and the shorter days of the year.

The Maya used two calendars, one for the civil or solar year, and another that was considered sacred. The civil year comprised 18 months with twenty days each which was 360 days total. In addition, there were five days of luck known as Uayeb which gave the total the same 365 days like our calendar. This year of 365 days was called haab. The sacred calendar was referred to as tzolhin It was comprised of the 260 days. The tzolliin days was the day of the rites of the people.

If we think of each year as revolving wheel, and a Tzolkin-day cog mingling with an haab-day-day cog, we can observe how Maya was aware of which day in the year of the ceremony was on which day of the year of civil war. Because the cogged wheels were constantly turning around, these two days would connect at least once every fifty years.

The nine divisions in time. These were:

kin-aday

Uinal- a month that is 20 days

Tun - a year that consists that spans 18.18 uinals (360 days)

Katun - 20 tuns which is equivalent to the equivalent of a year (7,200 days)

baktun - 20 katuns (144,000 days)

pictun - 20 bahtuns (2,880,000 days)

calabtun - 20 pictuns (57,600,000 days)

kinchiltun - 20 calabtuns (1,152,000,000 days)

alautun - 20 kinchiltuns (23,040,000,000 days)

The year time-divisions in the Maya are determined by the 20th number.

To learn about astronomy, the priests needed a second instrument to study astronomy: math. This time, they may have borrowed from the Olmecs however their accomplishments in this area are impressive. The Maya knew the importance of zero, which is zero. They also understood the concept of place-value notation, also known as mathematical arithmetic that is located in a particular position. We employ place-value notation whenever we write numbers in the present. For instance, if you put the word "one" in the form of (1) one (1), every zero that we add to the right will increase the number by ten times. 10, 100, 1,000.

The simplest version of Mayan writing numbers involved 3 symbols: the representation of an eggshell, or perhaps another symbol, to represent zero, dots; finally, the bar. The dot is one, and the bar is equal to five. Here's the number to 19:

It is believed that the Mayan method was called vigesimal, meaning, it was built on twenty. These numbers are read in a vertical fashion, starting from top to bottom and not horizontally. To get past nineteen, we need to consider groups of twenty.

We can read the final right-hand number in this manner There are 8,000 units in one, Two units of 400 equivalent to 800 7 units of 20 or 7 20 times 140; and then one bar or 5, resulting in the total 8,945. The number system is quite easy to understand, but the Maya also utilized head glyphs or images of heads that represented various numbers. For instance the head glyph that signifies the number 1 appears like this:

Head glyphs for the number 1.

The scholars can comprehend these bizarre head-shaped images but are in awe of the majority of the other Mayan Hieroglyphics. It is believed, however that the other glyphs are a record of the rituals of religious worship and ceremonies.

The Maya had a myriad of gods. The most important of them were Itzamna, God of the Heavens and of Day and Night. Chac God of the Four compass points. Chac, also known as the god of four compass points. Chac as well as Chacs were also gods of rain who brought rain by sprinkling water on gourds or caused flooding through throwing the gourds over when they got in a state of anger.

Other gods of note were Yum Kaax The God of Corn; Ah Puch, the God of Death; Ixchel, the Moon Goddess; Ixtab, the goddess of Suicide as well as a myriad of gods of the sky the sun, Venus, wind, heaven and hell along with the God of war, sudden Death and Human sacrifice. Additionally, there were gods to be worshipped throughout all seasons of the day.

It is believed that the Maya were of the belief that mankind was created from corn. The Maya also believed in the fact that earth was devastated several times by massive floods. There were 13 heavens and nine underworlds. The heavens and underworlds were divided into layers with a god to each level. The suicide victims went to the topmost level of heaven. People who were punished severely went to hell's lowest level known as Mitnal which was freezing cold.

Sacrifice was an integral part in Mayan religion during the latter time. Blood was an essential ingredient for gods, especially the gods of rain. Priests and commoners alike cut their ears and tongues and splattered their blood over the idols. It was believed that blood sacrifices could bring rain. Human sacrifices became more frequent during the final period during the Mayan empire. They occurred when disasters were afoot - for instance, during times of no rainfall, or when crops were not producing, or when plagues or foreign invaders or some other disaster hit. Usually, the sacrifices of humans were performed either through cutting or slicing the

The heart of the victim is removed by throwing spears of short length at a painted region on the chest of the victim or by throwing victims into cenotes which is a sacred well.

It is the Sacred Well at Chichen Itza was where humans were sacrificed to please the gods. The sacrificed victims fell sixty feet into the river below.

The most well-known Well of Sacrifice is located at Chichen Itza, where victims were thrown into deep, sacred waters that lie at a depth of sixty feet. This amazing ceremony drew hundreds of people from all across the globe. They came to watch the spectacular procession through Kukulkan's Temple of Kukulkan to the well's edge. The human sacrifices were never tied because it was believed to be as a privilege to have been selected to be part of the ritual. The ceremony was held in the morning and If the person was able to survive the fall and didn't drown before noon the victim was rescued from the water and asked to reveal what message he received by the deities. Whatever he said it was well-treated afterward because it was believed to be a part of God.

The Sacred Well at Chichen Itza has been dug up and bones of approximately fifty people have been discovered. The sacrifices were believed to be able to reach the highest heavens of the Mayan heavens.

In the same spirit-filled water the amazed Indians made gold jewelry such as jade beads, jade bells, copper bells and knives, as well as pottery as well as other treasures in order to be pleasing to the gods.

If the priest-rulers from two cities that were powerful fought and fought, war was often the result. War was usually fights after the crop was harvested, since the soldiers were farmers too. The war had two captains. The first, the nacom was elected for a term of three years while the second batab had his title for the rest of his life. Armed forces were established and trained within the villages. Some of the weapons used included spears as well as weapons of war, such as flint knives, war clubs the slings used to throw rocks and bows and bows and arrows. The Mayans also used a weapon that was secret that was used to throw in hornets' nests within the line of fire.

While the weapons were basic but the clothes were anything but simple. The warriors were painted on their bodies and had extravagant headdresses, feathered capses and jewelry. Drumsand horns constructed from conch shells provided additional sound to accompany their screams. The goal of war was the capture of prisoners, not kill them. The most important prisoners were sacrificed, while those who were not important became slaves. War usually ended when both party had enough prisoners and/or when time to plant.

4. TRANSPORT and TRANSPORTATION

The Maya were the best traders. Merchants, also known as ppolm Mayan was significant enough to get exempted from taxation.

Yucatan traders who traveled through the mountains of Guatemala brought their back obsidian, jade, as well as the feathers of the exquisite and rare quetzal bird, which was found only within the mountains that are part of Central America. Highland Maya traded honey salt, cotton, and a myriad of other things. The trade was not restricted exclusively to Mayan people as a whole. There was a town called Xicalanco situated on the west of the Yucatan Peninsula, was a trading hub for Mexican tribes like Toltecs as well as the Aztecs.

Due to frequent clashes between the city-states and merchants, they lived risky lives. A lot of them operated under the watchful eye and under the supervision of their private military or navy.

Trade was conducted across waters to the closer island of the Caribbean throughout the coastline of Yucatan and perhaps even as far south as Panama. Merchants had large canoes open which could reach as high as forty feet. the paddles were carried by slaves. The inhabitants of coastal cities like Tulum were farmers and fishermen. They traded dried fish, turtle eggs as well as conch shells.

The roads were wide and beautiful, connecting important cities. The roads were elevated from up to eight feet higher than the countryside. They were constructed of stone and were smoothed with lime cement and ran straight as arrows across miles. They were constructed and maintained by ordinary people. There were a few places of rest or wayside lodgings to rest tired travelers. They never experienced the wheel turning or the hoof's stomp as all travel was performed by feet. The Maya did not understand the concept of the wheel. Nor did they have horses or any other pack animals.

Since there was any pack animals anything transporting goods across the land was transported on the backs of the Indians typically over 30 or 40 miles. The entire family usually made the journey, even the youngest child was carried the burden of something.

The marketplaces were among the most important courtyards and plazas of the cities. Some of the more well-known of them is the Court of a Thousand Columns located at the foot of the Temple of the Warriors in Chichen Itza. The area is roughly four and one-half acres in size. There was a horde of people who likely purchased and bartered, traded, bargained, and argued over mountains of food items fruit meat, fishes tools pottery, animals feathers, birds - and even humans. Slave trading was a huge business. The slaves were typically unlucky prisoners of war, as well as people who had been residents of cities nearby.

While not all are standing, colonnades once enclosed the 40-acre open-air market in Cbicben Itza. The area situated at the base of the Temple of the Warriors, is sometimes referred to as"the Court of the Thousand Columns

There was no system of money like the one used in contemporary nations. Cacao beans were scarce and valuable, and were frequently used as currency. Quetzal-bird feathers, jade stone beads, slaves were also utilized as substitutes for money. The Maya also had counterfeiters. To deceive a client and/or merchant filled cacao bean shells that were empty with dirt. People who didn't wish to be taken advantage of had to learn to pinch or bite every bean to determine the firmness. Based on Bishop Landa who was a slave, a slave could yield one hundred cacao beans.

5. THE ARTS

The Maya were outstanding painters and sculptors, potters, and weaver. The most famous illustration of Mayan painting is found in The city of Bonampak that translates to "painted wall" In Mayan. (We are not aware of the origins of the city.) In 1946 Giles G. Healey was a photographer and researcher, discovered a house that was surrounded by three entrances and three spaces deep in the forest in the Usumacinta Valley. In each of the rooms, walls are adorned by murals, or paintings featuring beautifully attired priests and lords accompanied by servants; a stunning battle scene, elaborate ceremonies as well as dances, and an animal sacrifice. They were the first artefacts to depict Mayan life in plain language, without confusion caused by ornaments, flourishes and symbols. The vibrantly colored paintings were preserved for over one hundred years due to water slowly dripping across the roof of limestone, making a protective layer of lime on the walls.

In recent times, within a small ceremony-based city called Multunchic close to Uxmal and Kabah Similar wall paintings have been found. They are also images of scenes, not symbolic images.

In order to begin a mural the artist sketched the characters in red. After that, the background was painted. Then the specifics of the figure's clothing were added, and finally , each figure was drawn with black. The artists were experts at making paints made from minerals and occasionally , from plants.

The most well-known color is called Mayan blue. The origins of this gorgeous blue is not known. It is believed to have come from blue clay minerals. The pink and red colors were created by red iron oxide, yellows from ocher, dark browns from bitumen or asphalt and blacks carbon. The green colour was a result of mixing yellow and blue.

In the older cities, stone carving was all over the place. It is mostly made up of altars and stelae. Stelae - massive stones, the biggest of which is more than thirty feet high decorated with the image of a man, and are adorned with dates symbols. They were used as time markers and were built to be dedicated on the end of the katuns (twenty years) or half the katuns (ten years) and even hotuns (five years). Before the Indians created their designs into stone, they might have written their dates on wooden stelae. However, it is impossible to prove this because the wood was likely to have decayed in the past. There are wood-carved lintels that are affixed to the top of door openings. Masks and idols were created in wood. The most commonly used material for carving was sapodilla the robust chicle tree's wood.

In the more modern cities, the steps and walls of palaces and temples were adorned with sculptures of stone as and stucco models. Figures, faces, and glyphs were expertly made using a form of plaster, and later painted.

Gorgeous clay models are found in a graveyard on an island called Jaina. The small statues of women, priests and warriors, chieftains and others are exquisitely.

It's difficult to imagine that this high-quality pottery was made without a potter's tool however it is believed that it was. Mayan artists simply formed clay into lumps or took strands in their hands , and then wrapped around and round. When smoothed and shaped clay was transformed into a variety of things, including three-footed bowls and whistles that resembled the shapes of animals, platters incense burners, cooking pots as well as jars and vase.

Certain of these were painted, stamped or engraved, however many weren't. Then, some of the clay figurines appear to have been created in molds. Additionally, Mayan artists carved jade into jewelry and idols. Later they worked with metals, such as gold and copper.

The Maya enjoyed dancing and music however, these events were reserved for rituals of worship. Music was used as the backdrop to chant prayers, for telling the stories and myths of the people as well as for ceremonial dancing. There were no stringed instruments just wind instruments and percussion. Drums were made of hollow tortoise shells and logs and clay in any dimension and form. Other rhythm instruments were gourd rattles and bells and bones which were rubbed or tapped against one another. The bones of the human leg were employed to play the melody and rhythm. Flutes were also used to play the melody like trumpets, constructed from conch shells as well as wood and clay.

The music was more likely to be in tune than melodic, because it was a secondary function to dancing. According to Spanish sources when a dancer skipped one beat, the penalty was very severe. Dancers, often numbering hundreds, were penalized if they skipped an entire step. They had groups of male dancing as well as women however, the two seldom danced in a group. The ritual dances may have brought rain. Others portrayed the hunter and hunted. Other dances depicted the daily events and wars. According to the paintings at Bonampak dancers, they wore extravagant costumes. Maintaining a headdress that was three feet high and feathered dress in place during the war dance would be difficult, too.

The only instances of Mayan weaving are found, but the woven material is featured in murals and in carvings. However, within the Guatemalan highlands, weaving is being done as it was in the past as well many stunning objects closely resemble those depicted by the early people. The Maya were able to grow and process their own cotton and created their dyes themselves.

Another fascinating art form was the creation of feather mosaics. This involved weaving a variety of feathers in the fabric. In some cases, the feathers were secured with cords or glued on the fabric. Only priests, chiefs and the most powerful warriors could afford to have quetzal feather mosaics due to the cost. Jackets, helmets, and breechclouts were constructed from the quizal's gold-colored feathers. They were hung on poles with long lengths. feathers were also used to keep mosquitoes away and fleas away from nobles.

The Mayan sculpture is intricately-designed tattoos on the body, which was surely an art. The design was meticulously cut into skin and various dyes of different colors were applied to the cuts. It is likely that healing was an issue and the entire process should be painful. The patterns, which reflected the contours of the body and face were decorative, and even artistic, and could be more appreciated by the public than their owners.

6. THE CLASSICAL CITIES

Scholars can divide Mayan historical events in various different ways. We should only discuss those who belong to the Classical and Toltec or Post-Classical and Post-Classical Periods. It was the Classical Period drew to a near A.D. 850. In its time, the cities like Tikal, Copan, Piedras Negras and Yaxchilan became awe-inspiring. The same time was the period of greatest achievements: writing, arithmetic as well as astronomy arts were flourishing.

The most significant creations from the Maya were their cities. Classical Mayan cities weren't inhabited however they were the sites of rituals. The inhabitants lived outside of the city's boundaries at different locations, depending on their social status. Nearest to the plazas and temples were the houses of nobility and priests, next were the middle and merchant-class houses, and then were the homes of the peasants. There is no evidence of these homes has been discovered, as they were constructed out of perishable material, not made of stone.

Imagine thousands, if not hundreds of laborers moving, hauling or pulling tons of dirt and stone to create the massive earth platforms upon where the pyramid-temples were located. Many of the Mayan structures were constructed on the earth platforms. This monumental task was done without the assistance of draft animals or wheeled vehicles.

During the construction, seven-foot-high bonfires, with large pieces of limestone were set. The heat from these fires caused the limestone to create an aqueous powder, which was the primary ingredient in Mayan cement.

The slaves and farmers crowded the woods, cutting down trees to keep bonfires burning as at the construction site, the stone pyramid temple was built in its shape in its final form. Lime stucco or cement, was put on the stone blocks to make the stone surface extremely smooth. In some cities , the stones were cut prior to. In other places, the artisans employed only the stucco by modelling and shaping it into thousands of odd and gorgeous forms. Finally, the pyramidal Temple was painted.

Classical Mayan cityscapes were stunningly colored, but not as sparkling white or crisp gray as they are now. The elements and time have wiped away the exterior colors, however the vibrant hue is evident on many interior murals, and on numerous sculptured walls or steps and columns.

It is unclear the length of time it took to construct the pyramid-temple, however it was likely to take at least five years. In the meantime, the cities were being built or rebuilt repeatedly.

The temple that was completed was blessed by priests who committed it to the worship of a specific god. The temple was also dated according to the writing on the pictures of the Maya the same way that we engrave the date of completion on many of our bridges, structures and tunnels.

One might ask, what was the reason why these ancient people construct such beautiful cities if they didn't have a plan to live there? It is because they were constructed to please gods and to gain their favor.

A Tikal

In lower lands in Peten is the biggest city, possibly the oldest and certainly the most important out of the Mayan cities. The city was built on top of a lush green jungle, this city extends for several miles. The city's boundaries are not mapped. While archaeologists have been working in Tikal for a long time, the majority of Tikal is still unexplored. What look like hills that are covered in mosses, vines grass, trees and grass are actually temples and pyramids which are now buried maybe for eternity.

The stinging ants' columns move in a single line along the causeway made of stone; spider monkeys and parrots, as well as toucans and wild turkeys dominate the lush treetops of orchids. For the past twelve centuries, the sounds they've made have replaced those of singing priests and ceremonial dancers. The humidity and heat make it easier to increase within the rainforest and after the last Maya had left the town, jungle swept into the city quickly.

In 1696, the ruined Tikal was discovered in the hands of Father Andres Avendafio the Spanish priest who was a missionary for the Indians. The city is home to six enormous temples built in pyramids, two of which are located through a vast plaza. Temple of the Giant Jaguar Temple of the Giant Jaguar is the largest, and its pyramid is 16 stories tall. The top of the pyramid has an entrance that opens to three large rooms that are set one behind another. A massive roof comb, with a the crest of stucco and stone is added to the height and surely created the illusion of the temple to be more amazing in the eyes of those who were Mayan farmers.

The plaza's facing temple is decorated with artfully carved masks. It is referred to as"the Temple of the Masks, and is lower by twelve feet in comparison to Temple of the Giant Jaguar. Temple of the Giant Jaguar that is 143 feet in height.

This is known as the Temple of the Giant Jaguar located at Tikal. The temple has a beautiful roof comb, which depicts an erect high priest with enormous earplugs as well as an exquisite headdress. The temple was built about A.D. 750,

On the south-facing side of the plaza, there are the two rows of stelae. In between them is a five-step stairwell that extends across the plaza, leading to 16 more temples. The whole cluster of temples and pyramids is just one of the many of them in Tikal.

A tunnel was dug within Tikal's Temple of the Giant Jaguar opened up to a tomb that contained stunning pearl, jade, and shell jewellery, four inches high jade statue; many pieces of pottery painted with paint and an alabaster vase and a myriad of other precious offerings. It is expected that the treasures discovered at Tikal in each season of archeological excavation will aid in solving the many questions that remain about the Mayan civilization.

B, Copan

Around one hundred and twenty years ago the first archaeologist from the Maya arrived at the banks of the Copan River and "saw directly across a stone wall with furze growing from the top. Maybe a hundred feet high it ran from north to south along the River." John Lloyd Stephens, with his artist friend Frederick Catherwood, was looking at the second-highest Mayan cityof the Mayan, Copan. In awe of its forest-covered terraces with carved stelae and carvings, its stairs with sculptures and pyramids, Stephens purchased Copan for fifty dollars.

With a total area of more than seventy-five acres the city was a center of scientific research. Astronomers from the city determined the duration between eclipses. To commemorate their discoveries they constructed the shrine at the time of A.D. 756. It is among the three important structures within Copan's main section.

Another temple is dedicated our planet Venus. The third temple is located on high on the famed Hieroglyphic Stairway. There are sixty-two steps in the thirty-three-foot-wide staircase. Each riser is hand-carved and there are 2 000 hieroglyphic designs throughout the entire staircase.

While Mayan dates are decoded however, nobody is able to comprehend the carvings of characters. The middle of each 12th step is a massive standing statue of a god or priest as well as the ramp carvings to either side depict serpents with feathers.

Nearby is close by is the Nearby is the Jaguar Stairway. To either side are beautiful stone jaguars that were once covered with spots of shiny obsidian black.

The Hieroglyphic Stairway at Copan. John Lloyd Stephens thought that should the over two thousand glyphs found on the staircases could be read, they could reveal the whole story of the ancient city of Copan Copan is an elaborate maze of pyramids plazas and temples, surrounded by tiers of seats made of stone. A significant group of structures is situated seven miles from the central part. This suggests there was an area that was covered by an enormous amount of people.

In addition to being the hub of research, Copan was a great trading post. Being further south than similar Mayan cities, the city likely had a steady trade with the inhabitants of Panama and could also work using metals. Within the base of the stelae that was dedicated to the gods in A.D. 782, two tiny gold feet were discovered and separated by the figurine.

C Palenque

About three hundred miles to the north and west in Copan are the remains of Palenque. In 1952 in 1952, Palenque was discovered by Mexican archaeologist Alberto Ruz Lhuillier made a shocking discovery.

For more than four seasons, his crew had slowly removed tons of stone and earth from a staircase that was found under on the ground inside the Temple of the Inscriptions. They were now 60 feet lower, nearly to the foundation of the pyramid. Ruz was wondering what the reason was for the stairwell being blocked, and to where it went. A clue was in front of his eyes. There were the remains of six individuals. They could have been sacrificed in order to help a significant individual in the next life of his.

The men carefully worked making a cut through the rubble on the other end of a massive stone slab. Ruz was waiting impatiently until the hole became bigger. He then walked through it, and saw an ancient burial chamber that has not been seen in more than a thousand years.

The burial crypt is located beneath the Temple of the Inscriptions at Palenque

The water, which had been dripping down limestone for centuries, has formed sparkling crystals known as stalactites. In the walls of this haunting Chapel were nine stucco figures possibly representing those of nine deities from underworld. A carved stone slab nearly the same size as the 30-foot chamber was placed over an unfinished tomb. After the five-ton slab was gradually raised by workers and the polished stone tomb's lid opened up. Under it was the bones of the halach Uinic, which was covered by jade ornaments and an jade mosaic mask. Pottery, jade ornaments, and two stucco heads were discovered nearby.

The tomb could not be discovered had Ruz hadn't pondered the tiny holes in a flagstone that was found in the temple floor just from. These were finger holes in a secret trap door that opened onto the stairs.

From the tomb, the steps that led up to the first floor an unfinished tube made comprised of cement and stone. This pipe is likely employed by priests to transmit and receive messages from the priest-king who died below.

The Palenque pyramids had intricate roofs with elaborate combs. The wide doors and thin walls of the structures gave them a distinct advantage over those found in many Mayan cities. The walls were adorned with intricately carved or modelled figures of gods, rulers, animals, slaves, quetzals and mythical creatures. The art of stucco model-making reached its highest level.

It is the Temple of the Inscriptions at Palenque. A secret staircase inside the center of the pyramid leads to the famed burial site of the chieftain who was buried around A.D. 700

7. REVOLT, MIGRATION, AND THE TOLTECS

The huge Classical cities that were ceremonial in the Peten region were flourishing for more than 570 years. However, in A.D. 900 these centres were abandoned and were left to rot. Why? Archaeologists have offered a variety of possibilities to solve this mystery. Many have suggested that the soil would not provide enough food and that people had to move away from the area to be safe from the danger of starvation. Some have also suggested drought and earthquakes, as well as plagues or invasion, as well as extreme changes in climate.

Researchers have come up with a novel explanation. They think that the peasants revolted at the priests. Through the years, the priests' group had gotten bigger, as did the amount of rituals, gods and rituals. Priests had lost contact with the farmers, however the requirements they put on them been increasing. The work needed to be completed as well as more corn, more palaces and temples until finally the farmers regrouped. There's ample evidence to support this theory. A lot of buildings were abandoned half-finished and no more Stelae were built after A.D. 909.

The most convincing evidence could have been discovered within the towns in Tikal as well as Piedras Negras. A stela from Tikal was deliberately destroyed. A sacred throne and wall panel and stelae were destroyed in Piedras Negras. These items were once revered but reminding the people of their service. Blind faith turned to blind hatred.

The uprising took over. Priests and officials could have been executed. As time passed the peasants were without leaders. For centuries , they were instructed on what to do, and when, as well as how. Then they were on their own, with their new freedom. The temples were not being built. The jungle slowly grew into the plazas and the vines took over the steps of the temple. Then, gradually, the inhabitants left the cities.

Then comes a second mystery. What happened to the two million or millions of people? For a while, the scholars believed that they had migrated north into Yucatan and built new cities. However, it's now clear that the cities of the northern regions were already present and flourishing. It is possible that there are three possible answers to the mystery. Certain people continued to live their lifestyle, becoming less affluent and their numbers decreasing. Some emigrated into some of the Guatemalan highlands. Others moved north, to the Mexican states that are now known as Campeche, Yucatan, and Quintana Roo.

The major part of Mayan history shifted northwards towards a low range of hills called Puuc and an area known as the Yucatan plain. In the valleys and hills of the

Puuc region, were the stunning towns of Kabah, Labna, Sayil and Uxmal. To the north of the Puuc Hills and to the east were the city that included Mayapan, Dzibilchaltun, Izamal Chichen Itza, and Coba.

The Peten migrants had left behind the steaming rain forests, swamps as well as plains that were treeless and a complete revolution. They discovered the remnants of scrub, dense undergrowth growing out of a dehydrated plain, and a raging revolution in northern cities were struggling as well. The entire Mayan civilization was shaken to free it of the priesthood and it wasn't alone in this, as the agricultural tribes from in the Mexican mainland were attempting to achieve the same result. All over the Mayan country and in the Valley of Mexico, the Classical Period drew to a brutal end.

In the years following A.D. 900, most of the Maya resided in their native Guatemalan mountains or the northern Yucatan. The inhabitants of the highlands clearly did not advance their culture any further. People in Yucatan did, owing to Mexican invaders, known as the Toltecs.

Tula The capital of the Toltecs, was located 45 miles away from Mexico City. Prior to A.D. 900, the Valley of Mexico had come under the control of these ferocious and aggressive people. They used an astronomical calendar, were pyramid builders and engaged in many different crafts and arts. Through trade they came into Kontakt with Maya.

Carved on a the cliffs of Tula is a picture of Quetzalcoatl (ketsahl con-ahrl) as well as its designation Ce Acatl and a hieroglyphic date that dates the year A.D. 968. Quetzalcoatl is the title used by the Toltecs as a name for a god as well as to priest-kings. The Quetzalcoatl who revolutionized Mayan history was called Ce Acatl Topiltzin. Since legend and history have mixed up the story of the priest-king with that of the god with similar name, it is possible that we don't exactly what transpired. However, the chronicles of the past say that after 22 years as the ruler of the Toltecs the Toltecs exiled themselves and was followed by chiefs, priests as well as a small number of his own people.

The chronicles reveal that the emperor was in Mayan country between the time of A.D. 987 and 1000. The Maya appeared to have been unable to stand up to the invaders. The Maya were called Itza in the name of conquered tribe The Toltecs settled in Chichen Itza, "the well of Itza." In the meantime, Maya from and the Guatemala highlands were invaded around the same time.

What happened to Quetzalcoatl and Kukulkan the way his name was as in Mayan language, isn't well-known. Many believe that he floated away towards the dawn with a raft of interspersed snakes. As per legends, he vanished from the scene on Ce Acatl, the date when the date he was born. He promised to return on Ce Acatl.

In A.D. 1000, the Toltec warriors and priests had complete control over Yucatan The Quetzalcoatl who led the invasion had left. He was a sane thinker who could not have been a supporter of the bloodthirsty gods or priests, or the ceremonies that involved human sacrifice. Instead destabilizing the Mayan civilization in any way, the Toltec invaders brought life to the Mayan civilization.

The Toltec Quetzalcoatl is later Kukulkan. Mayan god Kukulkan. The background features an eagle-like serpent. Jaguars and feathered serpents are popular designs found in Toltec art.

8. CITIES of the North

Soon after the Toltecs gained control of the Maya and the Puuc region, they forced inhabitants of the Puuc region to relocate to the Yucatan plain, which was near the cenotes which are the natural pools in the limestone region. The T 01-tees likely believed to keep an surveillance of the farmers if they weren't scattered across their Puuc Hills. Additionally, the supply of water to the hill was always a issue.

The cities that were abandoned, Kabah, Labna, Sayil and Uxmal and Uxmal, as well as lesser-important cities, were ruined. The four Puuc cities were constructed close to each other. They were arranged, from north to south for about twenty miles, including Labna in from the west of Sayil. An estimated 25,000 people was once encircling them.

The remains of Puuc cities indicate that they were very distinct from the ones in the south and west. There are less pyramid-temples as well as a lot more palaces and a few stelae. The higher proportion of civic or royal buildings suggests a shift away clergy rule towards civil rule. Furthermore, the structures are typically constructed from concrete, and are topped with a veneer of exquisitely cut and fitted stones.

It is impossible to find anything in the Peten region that is comparable to the impressive palace at Sayil It has over 100 rooms. However, with windows that were dark and dark rooms were divided by stone walls and each room was tiny and damp. Instead of doors drop curtains or pull curtains shut their doors.

The curvature of the majority of Mayan rooms is due to the corbel arch. The sides slowly incline towards each other , and are joined by the capstone. An arch like this the roof could be a slaughter if the walls were set too in a space.

Corbel archway, with capstone

In Yucatan the Toltecs introduced the idea of putting an arch's vaulted ceiling on columns rather than dense, damp walls and rooms were made more spacious and airier.

A, Uxmal

The most stunning city in the Puuc region is Uxmal. The city's most prominent of the six major buildings includes The Palace of the Governor, as it was referred to by the Spaniards. The palace is located on an elongated terrace that is fifty feet in height, and covers an area of five acres. The building is wide and narrow, and has 24 rooms. The four sides of the building are decorated with around twenty thousand perfectly crafted stones Some of them weigh hundreds of pounds.

These exquisitely designed and arranged mosaic walls are among the finest works of art found in the Americas.

Just a few steps from the Palace is just a few steps away is the Nunnery Quadrangle. Here four buildings face a large court. Their elaborate walls made of carved and fitted stone portray rain gods serpents, latticework and many other things. The doors of the four structures are odd-numbered, namely five seven, nine and eleven.

Nearby is close by is the Pyramid of the Dwarf, or the House of the Magician, or the House of the Adivino. It is known with three different names. The intriguing pyramid is characterized by two rounded edges that make it oval. Its staircases are very steep.

The city plan of Uxmal

According to folklore of the natives, there was once a witch who was looking for an infant son. The witch was advised to place an egg from an iguana inside her home. This was done and within a few days the egg was able to hatch a beautiful baby boy. The happy witch raised her child with care however, when the handsome and brilliant child was eight years old, he did not grow anymore. After a while the dwarfed child of the witch was able to find an instrument of music within the woods. The idea was held by people that the person who could play the instrument could be the next King of Uxmal. When the dwarf began to play wonderful music on it every person in the city was able to hear the music. Naturally, the king who was reigning in Uxmal wanted to stay in the throne, therefore he challenged the dwarf to complete two duties. The first, the dwarf to prove his worth was required to build the largest most beautiful, fairest pyramid in all Uxmalwithin a single night. He did it; it is called the Pyramid of the Dwarf. Then three coconuts would be broken one after the next and placed on his head. If the dwarf was able to survive the king's cleverness, at the same time, was to be able to have three coconuts broken on his head.

Now , the witch had come up with a method of protecting her son, by making him a cap made of stone, on top of which she wore hair. Three coconuts landed onto the dwarf's head. Nothing occurred. However, the first bag to fall over the head of the king caused the king to death. The city's inhabitants were thrilled; they had an entirely new King. The magician-dwarf ruled them with wisdom throughout the years.

In the forest today, close to The Pyramid of the Dwarf in the area of the Pyramid of the Dwarf, is a statue that leans over an unattractive woman holding an animal. On the bottom of this sculpture is an extremely small silhouette who is crouching while the bag falls onto his head.

B, Kabah

Nine miles to the southeast from Uxmal is the second biggest Puuc city Kabah. In the past, an edifice linked these two cities. The arch of triumph located at Kabah is where it was built.

Three buildings have been cleared the scrub and earth at Kabah but many remain mounds. One of the most unique of the three are The Palace of the Masks, sitting on a platform that is low.

The facade of this structure are dozens of stone masks depicting the God of Rain Chac. The noses of all are large and coiled. It is shaped like one of elephants' trunks. A majority of these trunks were removed. Between A.D. 800 and 900, Kabah was probably surrounded by a lot of people. Due to the droughts of six months which were typical across the Puuc Hills, the Palace of the Masks might be constructed to serve as an "appeal made of stones" for Chac who was the God of Rain.

C, Sayil

Sayillies partially in two contemporary Mexican States: Yucatan and Campeche. The building with the most gorgeous design is the Palace is built on three levels with the highest two placed back as steps to terraces. The massive staircase is the first of 3 levels. The Palace walls are decorated with the Chac mask, as well as the gods that descend, as well as monsters sporting tails that resemble alligators. The columns are topped similar to those found in earlier Greece.

The stunning Palace located in Sayil isn't being renovated. The construction, which is common to the Puuc region, is made of concrete that is surrounded by tiny, finely cut stones.

Another temple, the Mirador is located on the the top of a tall pyramid. From the top, it is evident that almost all of Sayil's previous grandeur is now largely rubble.

D, Labna

The trunk-nose carving that is the deity Chac in Labna is an inscription that dates the time of A.D. 869. The city is famous because of its gorgeous Arch. In this arch, which is carved out of stone are the basic thatched homes from the Maya. On each side of the arch's entryway are two rooms. Nearby is a magnificent pyramid that has rounded ends and a temple that has an eaves and comb.

The Arch is located in Labnd. Roads connected the four major cities for ceremonies: Uxmal, Labna, Sayil and Kabah. The temple-pyramid that is visible in the background and crowned by a gigantic rooftop comb is known as the Mirador. The pyramid has rounded edges similar to Uxmal's House of the Magician at Uxmal has.

Labna Palace is located in the city of Hyderabad. Labna Palace is situated at the end of a ceremonial road that connects it to buildings around the Arch. The palace is actually a collection of buildings that were joined and constructed at various times. It was most likely Labna's state center. In the present, some spaces are utilized for guests staying overnight, since it is the sole sanctuary in miles of deserted, wild jungle.

e, Tulum

It is located in the eastern part located on the east coast of Yucatan, Tulum, unlike many Mayan cities was walled and fortified. In many areas, the walls were 20 feet thick and fifteen feet high and about eight hundred yards in length. In order to attack, enemies would have to cross the city via five gates that could have been protected by a handful of soldiers.

The city sits on a cactus-covered, high mountain that overlooks that of the Caribbean Sea. Its oceanfront is the Castillo which is the most significant construction at Tulum. The city and the temple are facing east. It is possible to picture the priests in Zama which was the name of Tulum's origins facing the sun's rising and chanting the gods' blessings to the coming day. Zama is "the sunrise" and Tulum refers to "walled."

The Castillo of the city walled of Tulum is located at the border of the Caribbean Sea

A stela is believed to date back to Tulum at least A.D. 564, but the city's history is largely inaccessible. In 1518, the crew of four Spanish ships led by Juan de Grijalva sighted the walls. One of the members of the expedition wrote "the Seville city Seville wouldn't have been as large or more impressive."

Two Spaniards who were shipwrecked from an earlier expedition had been taken for slavery Kinich Lord of Tulum who had a hard time escaping being slain and consumed. Two of them, Geronimo de Aguilar, was saved by Cortes while one of them, Gonzalo de Guerrero, was married to the Mayan chieftain's daughter, and was an honorary war captain. He took on the Indians in the battle against his countrymen.

Another significant structure located in Tulum includes The Temple of the Frescoes. The painted murals depict the gods of the rain and corn, as well as serpent designs, which are similar to those that were used by the Toltecs. Tulum is a city that has many things that are similar to the Mexican cities, despite the fact that it was founded in ancient times.

f, Dzibilchaltun

Nearly to the to the north of Merida the capital of the modern day of Yucatan is Dzibilchaltun. With its huge rubble mounds, excavators have discovered that the city was a time ago and very different from the cities of Puuc. Archeologists are currently working to restore Dzibilchaltun. Recently, they made a reconstruction of Dzibilchaltun's Temple of the Seven Dolls which was named so because seven clay dolls were discovered under its floor. Contrary to other Mayan temples it had windows.

There is also a nearby church that was built by the Spanish. It is constructed from many stones taken from the ruin of Dzibilchaltun and the tracetraces of Mayan images can be observed.

The Temple of the Seven Dolls located at Dzibilchaltun

9. THE MAYAPAN LEAGUE

The 11th century was when Itza established for their capital Chichen Itza, which was rebuilt three times. The Mayan inhabitants may have been at ease with the invaders since they assisted them in the construction. As time went by, Chichen came to look increasingly like Tula the capital city of the Toltecs.

The elaborate Toltec designs like warriors, jaguars and human skulls, and eagles were widely sculpted. The most important sign of Toltec influence, though, was the serpent column, symbol of Quetzalcoatl-Kukulkan.

The Itza The Itza ruled Chichen for approximately two centuries, from A.D. 987 to 1185. Native accounts say that this was the period when the League of Mayapan. Cities-states such as Uxmal, Chichen Itza, and Mayapan were believed to have ruled together over Yucatan,

However, at this time there is no an accurate picture of Mayan time and its history. Archeologists claim that Uxmal was already abandoned, and Mayapan was built following Chichen was destroyed. There are some theories that Izamal and not Uxmal might be the third city of the alliance of triple cities.

The famous columns of the feathered serpent at the at the top of the pyramid that bear Cbicben Itza's Temple of the Warriors at Cbicben Itza Since the feathered serpent is an Mexican image, we can confirm that these bizarre columns were constructed following the Toltec Snoaston.

The Books of Chi lam Balam offer us a fascinating story of an unimportant chief with the name Hunac Ceel. This young man was witnessing an act of sacrifice on Chichen Itza's Sacred Well in Chichen Itza.

The entire morning, the peaceful locals and priests remained at the edge of the well in anticipation of the return of the victims who had been sacrificed. The dark waters were quiet since the dawn and no one was back with a word from gods. Then Hunac Ceel ran towards the temple's platform and threw himself into the water 60 feet below. A few seconds passed, the crowd was stunned, motionless then Hunac came back. Hunac was removed out of the water by the holy words were spoken by the Gods to make him King. Then, he decided to choose Mayapan as his capital city.

The tale continues to state that the chief of Chichen Itza, a certain Chac Xib Chac, stole the bride of Ah Ulil, chief of Izamal. Hunac Ceel gathered a huge army and attacked Chichen. Chac

Xib Chac was driven out and Chichen was thrown down, but did not be seen again.

Based on the stories, Hunac is a daring plotter. After he was successful in defending Ah Ulil's honour, Hunac turned on his Allies which led to Ah Ulil and Izamal both fell. Hunac's strength lies in his band of Mexican bodyguards, who were equipped with a deadly new weapon which was the bow and an arrow.

The Lords of Chichen Itza and of Izamal were forced to reside at Mayapan in the form of hostages and had some power. The Cocom named after the name that Hunac was the name given to his dynasty was the ruler of Yucatan for approximately two hundred and fifty years. Mayapan was at the time the first city that was truly capitalized by the Maya. It was a fortress walled city and was inhabited instead of being just a town of temples. The inhabitants of the city were not supported so much by agriculture, but through the remuneration made by Mayan people. In a space of just two miles, 15000 people resided in thirty-five hundred structures.

The wall around Mayapan was 12 feet in height and was often as thick. In the city, there were numerous cenotes (wells) and the homes of the nobles were near the cenotes. The city's center was a replica from The Temple of. Kukulkan located at Chichen Itza, its four sides which were facing the cardinal points on the compass. The residences that belonged to the families of power were situated close to that plaza.

Mayapan included the most shabby evidence of Mayan architecture as well as the ugliest pottery. The low number of temples suggests that the religious beliefs had fallen to an unsustainable level. Constructions were made of poorly cut stone and errors were covered with thick layer of stucco. The stones were sometimes placed in mud. Today, Mayapan remains mostly old rubble. What remains is that the structures appear to be poor copies of the ones found at Chichen.

a, Chichen Itza

Contrasting from Mayapan was the beautiful Chichen Itza, a city that was beautiful Chichen Itza. Chichen Itza has seen a lot of restoration work was completed by archeologists, and we can now see how amazing this city could have been.

It is believed that the Temple of Kukulkan rises majestically from the flat plain of Yucatan. The sides of the temple are a tribute to the past. There are four staircases, each of which has ninety-one steps. Four times ninety one is 364 when you add the top level of the platform provides us with 365, which is that's the amount of days of the year civil. Nine terraces in the pyramid were divided into fifty-two panels, which is the appropriate amount for the Toltec calendar of the ceremonial. Additionally, the terraces were divided by stairs into 18 sections, which is which is the number of months of the Mayan year.

Within the Kukulkan pyramid, there is another pyramid that has one room that was secret, and included one of the most famous Red Jaguar Throne. The stone was huge. jaguar was painted in red and once contained seventy-three jade spots that were polished.

Chapter 14: Religious Practices

Religion was a major aspect in Mayan culture. Archeologists could gain insight into their practices of religion, that were based on the ancient Mayan codices, including the Popol Vuh, the Paris Codex and the Madrid Codex.These could be the last texts discovered to survive the massive loss of Mayan texts by the Spanish friars.

It is believed that the Mayans believed in numerous nature gods that lived in a realm of the supernatural. They believed that certain gods were believed to be stronger and thus more significant over other gods. To please the gods they Mayans constructed pyramids, participated in rituals, and paid them a ceremonial homage.

Apart from gods In addition to gods, they Mayans were also fond of worshiping their dead ancestral ancestors. The reason for this was the conviction that the ancestors of their past would aid them in communicating with gods. The Mayans even placed their deceased relatives under the floors of their homes because they believed that the deceased would watch over their people.

They believed in gods. Mayans believed in god-like rulers and believed that they played the role of intermediaries between mortals and gods. This belief was propagated by the ruling elite who profited from the religious nature of people by making themselves gods to justify their right to rule.

Apart from being the ultimate king of God, priests or shamans also served as mediators in order to please the gods. Priests were drawn from the most prestigious social class and played various tasks. The most significant was to conduct rituals that called for rain as well as to prevent drought, famine and earthquakes. These ceremonies included incense burning and ritual dances bloodletting, ritual dance, and even sacrifices of the human body. They also portrayed the gods, make magical acts, and even predict the future. They also had the responsibility of making tables for eclipses. The roles of these were detailed within the Books of Chilam Balam, particularly in the Book of the Jaguar Priest.

Human Sacrifice

There was a belief that Mayans were of the belief that gods were fed by blood as the primary source of power. That is why it was believed that the death of any living creature was considered to be the greatest sacrifice of devotion. The decapitation ritualistic of soldiers of honor, particularly the king who was in conflict was believed to be the most significant sacrifice ever (captive commoners were not usually sacrificed but rather placed in the pool of labor).

Prior to the decapitation ceremony the victim was initially assaulted, burned, tortured or cut in the evisceration process. It was in the time between the Classic and Post-Classic Periods that heart extraction was practiced by the Mayans in the manner inspired through the Aztec neighbors. Heart extraction was performed on the summit of a pyramid or inside the inner courtyard of the temple. In certain rituals, the shaman would wrap the body of the victim but leave the feet and hands unharmed. The shaman would then remove his ceremonial attire and put it over the skin. Following that, he'd dance as a symbol of resurrection.

Astronomy

In the past, Mayans believe that the heavens was composed of thirteen levels while that the world beneath it, Xibalba, consisted of nine levels. Earth or "the mortal world," was located between heaven and underworld.

The earth was thought to be a massive wheel that was surrounded by divine waters, orteoatl. Above it was the first heavenly level wherein resided the clouds as well as the moon. It was calledilhuicatl metzli. In that layer over it was thecitalco. It was the place of the fixed stars as well as the goddessCitallicue. Next was the level the place where the sun, called orilhuicatltonatiuh, resided. In the fifth level , there was the "Great Star"" also known as Venus, the celestial being the Mayans were able to turn to in the context of conflict. In the sixth level, it was calledIlhuicatl Mamalhuazocan. It is a reference to "Heaven of the Fire Drill" and could actually comprise from the Orion's Belt along with comets (which were believed by the Mayans believed were fire serpents responsible in bringing the sun to toward the east). The seventh layer was where the powerful winds and storms resided. The next level was the one with dust and was considered to be the "blue sky." Beyond that was the level referred to as theitztapal nanatzcayan. It translates to "where stones collide," and it was the place where thunder ruled. The three levels over it were represented by the hues red, white and yellow. The topmost level was known as theomeyocan and was believed to be the home of the god of hermaphrodite who created space and time lived.

For the Mayans the movements from celestial entities were gods' method of communicating with them. For the interpretation of these messages the Mayans used the term theilhuica tlamatilizmatini which translates to "the wise person who studies the skies." These were the Astronomers that studied the sky in order to make "predictions" for the future. Every day, at dawn the Mayan astronomers surveyed the skies, and then recorded the patterns they saw in the form of codices. These records played an important contribution to the growth of Mayan civilization, specifically in the field of agriculture.

Mythology

In spite of the destruction and destruction the old Mayan texts by Spanish conquistadors thePopol Vuh, also known as thePopol Wujby known as the K'iche' Mayans were able to survive.Popol Vuhis was translated as the "book that the people of this community" and it recorded the genealogiesand land rights, as well as mythology from the early colonial Mayans from the K'iche' royal Scribes. One of these tales describes the creation of the universe according to the Mayans.

Mayan Story of Creation Mayan Story of Creation

In the beginning, before all things were made of darkness, silence, as well as water, it was believed that there existed seven gods. They all resided in the depths of the ocean and were covered in feathers of blue-green. One god was the serpent with feathers, Kukulcan (and his Aztec nickname is Quetzalcoatl). Other gods were referred to in the form of the Framer along with Tepeu, the Shaper, Tepeu, and Xmucane and Ixpiyacoc who were the godparents in Mayan mythology.

Together with Hurakan also known as Heart of Sky Together with Hurakan, also known as Heart of Sky gods created Earth (the Mayans believed that the earth was formed by the gods in the year 3114 B.C., therefore making this the "zero" date on Mayan calendar). Mayan calendar).

But they still wanted to make a distinction between the sky and the earth, so they established a siba tree in order to provide space for all living creatures that would be on the earth. It is believed the roots of its tree were placed in such a depth that they could surpass all levels that comprised the Mayan underworld, Xibalba, and its branches were so high that they surpassed all thirteen of Mayan heavens.

When the Ceiba tree was planted, gods then made the plants, and were followed by animals. However, the animals couldn't nor speak, or even be worshiped, and so the gods chose to make humans with hearts and minds that worship them and "keep the hours."

The gods initially tried to make human beings from the mud, but it proved to be unsuccessful as they never had souls or the capacity to endure the day. To take them down and start fresh, the gods caused an immense flood.

The gods once again attempted to do it again by creating human beings made of wood. But, the wooden human could not worship which is why they destroyed them and began the process over. A few of the wooden human were able to survive they could be people who were the ancestors of the monkey.

At this point an individual named Xquic who was the granddaughter of one of the nobles from Xibalba spoke to the head cut off by Hun Hunahpu which was put on display against the tree's trunk. tree. Hun Hunahpu's name was not disclosed in the text and there was a belief that he had been murdered by the Lords of Xibalba. In the course of their conversation, Hun was a spitter on Xquic's hands and made her pregnant with Hunahpu and Xbalanque and later were referred to as the powerful Maya Hero Twins.

When twins became born there no moon or sun and only the earth and the sky. A bird called the Seven Macaw proudly claimed as the sun as well as the moon, however this was not the case. This was because the Mayan Hero Twins shot the Seven Macaw with darts.

Twins also were renowned as a formidable ball player and wanted to utilize this to help bring their dad Hun back to his former glory. They attempted to do this by inviting the lords of Xibalba for a game of ball match however, the lords were enforcing one requirement, and that is that twins must first be able to overcome the gruelling challenges before them in Xibalba. The twins, obviously weren't viewed as heroes in the future for the sake of. With their wit and skill they were able to prevail in the game and that allowed them to be able to see their father revived.

When he rose again, Hun became known as Hun, the Maize God. For those who were the Hero Twins, they climbed back down to earth from Xibalba and continued to ascend into the sky to become the sun and moon. The sun's light and moon allowed gods to grow the fields of yellow and white corn and later could use to create a brand new human-like form. The first time, it was successful and, as a result humans were able to walk on earth.

The Mayan Gods

Kukulcan the serpent with feathers god

Mayans were a religion that worshipped numerous gods, but the most important was Kukulcan the serpent that was feathered. There was a belief to be that Kulkulcan was the god that instructed the Maya the different art forms of civilization, and imparted to them knowledge of medicine, agriculture, law and fishing.

Kukulcan was a deep-sea creature who lived in the ocean, and after his visit to Earth to impart his knowledge to people, returned to the ocean. The ancient Mayans consider that Kukulcan will return on Earth through the East and, if that occurs it will signal the end of the world.

It is interesting to note it is believed that Hernan Cortes de Monroy and Pizarro was the Spanish conquistador was believed by Aztec Empire's the governors Tendile as well as Pitalpitoque to represent the embodiment of Kulkulcan and was the fulfillment of the prophecy.

Itzamna is the god of fire.

Itzamna was the most significant Maya god, as the belief was that he made the world. He ruled the heavens including night and day. It was believed that the Mayans believed that they had him as the one who created their writing system, as well as the renowned Mayan calendar.

The god of storms.

Huracan also known under the other name Bolon Tzacab is the Mayan god of storms. According to legend that he created the great flood that washed away the Mayans who were angry with the gods.

Chaac is the god of thunder and rain.

Chaac was a god of great importance to the Mayans as, in addition to being the god of thunder and rain He was also a symbol of fertility and agriculture. In Mayan art it was depicted like an older man sporting hairy eyes, a nose that was long and amphibian or reptile body parts. Eyes were dripping with tears in some paintings, possibly to signify rain. A few of them also indicated the axe he used that he used to make thunder.

Even to this day, some Mayan farmers continue to seek out Chaac for blessing their fields. From the beginning the man was calledAh Tzenul, meaning "he who gives generously food to people,"Ah Hoya, which means "he who vomits," andHopop Caan,or "he who illuminates the sky."

Yum Cimil

Ancient Mayans were believed to have the god of death Yum Cimil, who was also known as Ah Puch. It was the god who was the god of the underworld of Xibalba. Yum Cimil was an esoteric body, and decorated himself with bones and a neck collar made from eye sockets. There were paintings that showed the body of Yum Cimil with black spots to symbolize rotting flesh.

Yumil Kaxob, the other god of maize

The god of maize Yumil Kaxob is depicted in paintings of an innocent young man wearing an elaborate headdress made of maize, and was depicted with a curly streak across his cheek. As opposed to the other gods Yumil Kaxob was not powerful. He was believed to depend on the god of rain to guard him from the god of death who was the one responsible for famine and drought.

Yum Kaax The god of agriculture and nature.

Yum Kaax was thought by many to be the incarnation of Maize and was believed to be the keeper of wild beasts. The hunters of the past rely on Yum Kaax to guide them as they believed he knew the songs that would guarantee them to succeed in hunting.

Kinich Ahau, second sun god.

Another sun god by Kinich Ahau, was worshipped by Mayans especially in the Itzamal city. Itzamal. It it was thought that the god would come to Itzamal every day at noon as macaw. The people would make offerings to him for consumption when he visited. In art Kinich Ahau's image is shown as having dental whitening, which represents the jaguar.

Ixtab is the suicide goddess

In the past, Mayans believed that the act of dying could bring one to heaven. They believed in the god of suicide Ixtab whom was depicted as a woman wearing a an untied rope in her neck. The Mayans believed they were Ixtab who was the one who took their souls to heaven after their death.

It is worth noting that upon the arrival of Spanish conquistadors the majority of the prehistoric Mayans were unwilling to surrender, and instead took their own lives.

Ix Chel The rainbow goddess

Ix Chel Was the goddess patron of weavers and pregnant women. The story of how she got her name is filled with sorrow.

Ix Chel was obsessed in the god of sun. However, this led her grandfather to be furious with her to the point that she was able to be killed. He struck her with a lightning bolt and instantly killed her. When her body was lying dead upon the earth, dragonflies swarmed and sang for a total of one hundred and three days. Then she awoke and be taken to the palace of the sun god.

But, the sun god was an unrepentant lover. The sun god believed Ix Chel as well as his brother, the dawn star were involved in an affair. His jealousy caused him to exile Ix Chel out of the sky, only to later return her. This was a source of irritation for Ix Chel and she made the decision she'd have to remain invisible when the sun god appeared in his face.

The result was that she was forced to live in perpetual evening hours in a watchful manner, caring for women that were pregnant and taking care of them while they gave birth.

Political and Social Life

From the very beginning of Mayan civilization, there was always been a clear line drawn between the wealthy and the commoner. As their communities expanded as well, their political and social structures became more complex as well. It is possible that a middle-class was in existence during at the time of the Classical Period, and it could have included low-level priests, officers, warriors artisans, merchants and officers.

Mayan civilization could be comprised of more than 90% commoners. They were mostly composed of laborers, farmers servants, slaves, and farmers. But, there aren't enough records to provide any information about their personal histories and lifestyles. They lived in homes constructed of non-perishable materials and placed on low platform. Commoners had to pay taxes and were also responsible for the production of products for the elite, as well as to consume for themselves, including cacao and cotton, as well as ceramics, and so on.

The land may have been occupied by clans, and passed on over generations. The lands were later amalgamated into city-states, each of which had an sovereign government and was led by the King. The city-state contained one main city at its center and was covered by smaller towns and settlements.

Royal Culture

Classic Maya art was filled with evidence of royal culture during the ancient Mayan civilization. It is clear that the King was thought of as a god-like ruler which was typically depicted as the embodiment of the maize god who was young and whose shoulders were the foundations for the civilisation. The lesser lords under monarch's reign were known as theajawand and were part of the council. Governors of the regions and captains of war were known as thesajal. The word means "feared the one."

The right to inherit the throne is patrilineal particularly to the oldest son. Young princes were referred to as ch'ok, which originally means "youth." This word was later made to refer with a noble all over the world. Apart from being the successor to the throne any potential king must become a respected war chief and the reason for this was the amount of captives they were able to capture. Only way for women to succeed as the head of an entire city would be in the event that the dynasty did not have an heir male and was at risk of dying.

In order to crown a new king the elaborate ceremony was performed at the top of an altar. The sacrifice of a human being was performed to honour the new King. As part of the ceremony, he was also given the crown jewels, embellished with a jade piece and quetzal feathers. It also included the royal scepter. It represented Chaac or K'awiil, god of maize. A few evidences showed that there were instances when the face of the king had his attendants covering it when confronted by the people of the commons. This could be due to boost their belief in the divinity of his king.

Political Administration

It was also the core of the Mayan political administration , and the selection to officials wasn't a matter of bureaucracy but rather a hierarchical process. The officials were most elite of society, and usually were promoted to higher ranks in the official ranks while they continue to serve as the head of the royal court. They made a promise to be"the "property" to the patron even if the sponsor's death. The only non-elite officials of the court of royals were tax collectors from local districts. They were known as thelakam.

Law

The Mayan governments imposed strict rules on the population. Certain crimes like murder, sacrilege, or arson could be punished with death. However they weren't exempt of the law, since if the crime was proved to be accidental or a mishap, the punishment was diminished. Additionally, nobles and commoners alike were not exempt from the law. In some instances, the case of a noble being indicted, he might be subject to a greater punishment than an ordinary citizen.

It is important to note that the imprisonment of criminals could not have been the norm in Mayan civilisation. Instead, if someone was punished for his crime and was punished, it could range from fines, through slavery, and even death.

If a citizen violated an act of law, the person in question was brought before the tribunal where the nobles or officials served as judges. There were cases where the king himself was judge.

Conclusion

Thank you so much for purchasing this book!

I hope this book is helpful to discover more about the amazing Mayan people, why they were them so unique and advanced and why they experienced decline. The world is constantly discovering new knowledge. Discovered that allow us to rethink our understanding of ancient civilizations including Maya. Mayan people. The new information brings higher level of understanding. This book is designed to offer a greater level of knowledge to all those who are interested in Mayan culture. Mayan people.

There is plenty to be learned from the past even though it appears disconnected from our current world. We're always in touch with our past, regardless of how long it takes. Everything we enjoy and appreciate in the present time has its roots in the past times, and so gaining knowledge about the people who lived back then could provide useful knowledge. It is also possible to discover where the ancient civilizations made mistakes and got wrong, and apply this knowledge to improve our lives as well as the world that surrounds us. It is my wish that you were enthralled and energized by this book.

Thanks for your kind words and good luck!

www.ingramcontent.com/pod-product-compliance
Lightning Source LLC
Chambersburg PA
CBHW050406120526
44590CB00015B/1844